Praise for *Broken*

"It has been a privilege to collaborate with Paul LeBlanc on several occasions around the issue of climate change. There the innovative motivation of education met with the inspirational tradition of the church. In *Broken*, we once again acknowledge and admire the parallel worldview of the church in Paul's approach to 'dreaming bigger dreams' (what in theological jargon we would call the heavenly kingdom), 'the power of stories' (what in the Christian Gospel we observe in the parables), and 'the heart of leadership' (what in church language is conveyed by an 'episcopate' that looks beyond the conventional). It's an invitation to imagine different dimensions of the same challenges, abandoning old tired ideas and reaffirming the most important human and spiritual values. That is why this book deserves wide readership and recognition."
—His All-Holiness Ecumenical Patriarch Bartholomew

"We are navigating a world filled with broken systems. But in the wreckage lies opportunity. In his powerful book *Broken*, Paul LeBlanc outlines what a world that centers our shared humanity can look like, and why it's so critical that we seize the chance to make bold changes—now. This is requisite reading for anyone who wants to be a part of the solution, not the problem."
—Jacqueline Novogratz, CEO, Acumen and Author of *The Blue Sweater* and *Manifesto for a Moral Revolution*

"As I dove deeper into *Broken*, I was encouraged yet also more impatient in regards to the need to unleash Paul's 'systems of care' in addressing many of today's social justice problems, especially the educational divide. As Paul intimates, how do we build social systems that 'love ALL those they are intended to serve?' *Broken* inspires those who are already engaged in education and/or social justice movements, as well as those who are on the sidelines, to find a compelling 'why' to find equity-centered solutions. You'll find yourself hanging onto every word. Another must read from Paul."
—Janiece Evans-Page, CEO, Tides

"Paul LeBlanc, one of the nation's most innovative and visionary university presidents, offers a thoughtful and thought-provoking look at how to counter the despair so many Americans feel about the state of our most vital systems—from education to health care to criminal justice. For all of us eager to find ways to truly be the change, *Broken* is a worthwhile and inspiring read."
—Thasunda Brown Duckett, CEO, TIAA

"Paul does a masterful job of honestly assessing our social systems from higher education to health care and criminal justice, weaving in his own decades-long personal and professional journey. He boldly posits that we are all complicit in broken systems that often fail those they are intended to help; but, instead of pointing fingers and laying blame, Paul lays out a strong case for how each of us can play a role in delivering on our promise to all people to help them realize their highest potential. As a CEO and workforce expert, I have a newfound appreciation for the national and economic security implications of not having a prepared workforce and too many people left behind, which is why *Broken* is such an important work."

—Johnny Taylor, CEO, Society for Human Resource Management (SHRM)

"In his last book, Paul LeBlanc challenged us to think differently about opportunity and access to college. In his galvanizing new book, LeBlanc turns his attention to systems of care in our society, including health care and criminal justice, in addition to higher education, that are in a state of brokenness. Employing his considerable gifts as a storyteller, LeBlanc asks his readers to consider social systems informed by love and respect for the human condition. LeBlanc helps us to conceive of a more whole and more humane society."

—Dr. Matthew G Biel, Division Chief and Vice Chair
for Child and Adolescent Psychiatry, Georgetown
University Medical Center—Medstar Health

BROKEN

Also by Dr. Paul J. LeBlanc

Students First: Equity, Access, and Opportunity in Higher Education

BROKEN

HOW OUR SOCIAL SYSTEMS ARE FAILING US

AND HOW WE CAN FIX THEM

DR. PAUL J. LeBLANC

Matt Holt Books
An Imprint of BenBella Books, Inc.
Dallas, TX

Matt Holt is an imprint of BenBella Books, Inc.
10440 N. Central Expressway
Suite 800
Dallas, TX 75231
benbellabooks.com
Send feedback to feedback@benbellabooks.com

BenBella and *Matt Holt* are federally registered trademarks.

Printed in the United States of America
10 9 8 7 6 5 4 3 2 1

Library of Congress Control Number: 2022013476
ISBN 9781637741764 (hardcover)
ISBN 9781637741771 (electronic)

Copyediting by Ruth Strother
Proofreading by Marissa Wold Uhrina and Brock Foreman
Indexing by WordCo Indexing Services, Inc.
Text design and composition by PerfecType, Nashville, TN
Cover design by Paul McCarthy
Cover image © Shutterstock / Suradech Prapairat (plate); © Shutterstock / CRStocker (gears)
Printed by Lake Book Manufacturing

Special discounts for bulk sales are available. Please contact bulkorders@benbellabooks.com.

For my parents, Eugene and Delphine, who taught me that every person deserves respect and a helping hand when in need.

CONTENTS

INTRODUCTION

I have worked in higher education for all of my adult life, but this book is not about higher education. Nor is it a memoir. It's about how we can put people back at the center of systems that ostensibly exist to serve them but so often fail them instead—often miserably so. That realization arose for me when I was writing *Students First: Equity, Access, and Opportunity in Higher Education*, a book about how to fix our system of higher education, the system I know best. That book, published in 2021, covers system redesign, better ways to measure performance, alternative ways to structure financial aid, and other attributes that shape our system of higher education. If we are to fix that system, we have to look hard at the way it is structured—at the policies, technologies, organizational structures, and operating assumptions that constitute the whole.

The goal of that analysis seems obvious: to make the system work better for students. Yes, higher education exists for many reasons: to create new knowledge, serve the economy, prepare the workforce, and provide entertainment. But its raison d'être is educating learners so they can improve their lives, nurture their families, and serve their

1

communities. As such, the system should reflect a devotion to—dare I say *love for*—students.

However, for too many Americans, the system inflicts a kind of emotional, psychological, and even material violence. Consider a system that

- fails 45 percent of those who enter but never complete a degree;
- saddles students with $1.7 trillion of debt, more than any form of debt aside from home mortgages;
- creates anxiety and even depression among high school students worried about the admissions process;
- forces students to conform to the system's demands rather than build in system flexibility to meet individual student needs;
- exploits student-athletes to serve a multibillion dollar entertainment business in which they share almost none of the wealth they create, while their football coach routinely is the highest paid person on campus; and
- favors those who already enjoy prosperity and privilege, while perpetuating inequities and failing low-income students, especially students of color.

Does this sound like a system that loves its students, the people it is supposed to serve? Ironically, higher education is full of people who care deeply about students and who come to their work with a sense of calling. Yet it routinely fails its students, is viewed with diminished regard by Americans, and is frequently seen as a problem for our society, not part of the solution.

That same argument can be made for other systems in our society, systems ostensibly designed to serve people in critically important ways but routinely fall short. I have many friends working in health care who were drawn to their professions by a desire to help, heal, and even save people, but who now serve a system that fails Americans in myriad ways. Millions of Americans do not have easy and affordable access to high-quality health care. We pay more for our prescription drugs than any other country, and low-income citizens often make trade-offs between food, rent, and the medicine they need to survive. Our bankruptcy courts are filled with cases of uninsured people sunk by medical bills. Parts of our country have infant and maternal mortality rates more typical of underdeveloped economies.

I also know many people who work in the criminal justice system—from police officers to judges—who came to their careers with a sense of calling but are now part of a system that imprisons and executes more people as a percentage of the population than any other economically developed country; that includes the failed War on Drugs effort, resulting in mass incarceration of people of color and the devastation of Black communities; that embraces a militarized and armed response to basic human problems of mental health and addiction and poverty; and that perpetuates structural racism.

Our government is full of people who take quite seriously their role of public servant and see their work as a kind of civic duty. During a sabbatical, I worked in the US Department of Education and met scores of people who care deeply about their responsibility to the American public good. Yet we have a democracy that is teetering for a variety of reasons, and the public worries about the government's ability to do good work, its enormous waste and inefficiency, and the corrosive influence of deep-pocketed special interests.

How often do people positively describe their interactions with the bureaucracies of higher education, health care, the criminal justice system, or government? Conversely, people who started working in

3

those systems with a genuine desire to improve lives now feel besieged, unsupported, and demoralized. For far too many people who work in or are served by these systems, a kind of dehumanization has set in. And not always for lack of investment, either. The US spends enormous sums on these systems—$3.8 trillion on health care,[1] $182 billion on prisons,[2] and $632 billion on higher education[3]—and yet they routinely fail us.

When we seek to improve these systems, our efforts focus on policy debates, technical solutions, funding, and data. While these are important, this book explores what is required to put core human questions back at the heart of our distinctly human-serving systems, what I call systems of care. I originally set out to answer the question of what it would take for my industry, higher education, to love its students again. But my inquiry expanded to ask that question of all systems of care. Not in a customer service sense, though that would help, too. I became increasingly focused on more existential questions, prompting me to explore topics like mattering, aspiring, storytelling, and, yes, even loving.

My reflections on those topics borrow heavily from my experience in higher education, the system I know best, and from my life. For those lessons to have context, and so I won't have to provide background each time it comes up, I will share a little about my journey. However, I include throughout the book stories and insights from colleagues in other industries and systems because the questions are as central to those other areas as they are to my industry. Indeed, they are the most important questions we can ask as we try to fix a broken America that is failing far too many of its people. *A note about the text: while published sources are cited, my recorded conversations with the many amazing people I interviewed during the course of my research are not. The excerpts from those recorded interviews are simply presented as conversation with no associated citation.*

My Story: The Professional Journey

I fell in love with teaching when I was a teaching assistant in the English department at Boston College, where I studied for my master's degree. It was an eleventh-hour appointment, just days before the start of the fall semester, and provided free tuition and a modest stipend. It felt like winning the lottery. I was handed a pile of books to teach and assigned a couple of sections of freshman composition, the mandatory first-year writing class for all incoming students. Ten minutes before the very first class I was to teach, I broke the zipper on my pants. I rushed to the classroom and sat behind the desk for that whole first hour, no doubt worrying my students that I was not a very dynamic instructor. That inauspicious beginning notwithstanding, I discovered a love for teaching, took joy in my students, and had that exhilarating sense when one discovers what one is supposed to do in this life. I would be an educator.

To do that and compete for a full-time academic job, I needed a doctorate. So I went from BC to the University of Massachusetts at Amherst, where I once again taught in the writing program. After completing my doctorate, I landed a faculty position at Springfield College as an assistant professor of English. I pretty quickly became department chair and grew active in campus governance and politics, serving as the faculty senate president during a contentious period when the college rid itself of a failed president.

At the same time, I was working with a lot of the emerging technologies of the 1990s, writing about ways to harness those technologies in teaching, learning, and publishing. That work came to the attention of Houghton Mifflin Company (now Houghton Mifflin Harcourt), one of the large textbook publishers trying to make sense of new technologies for its industry. Houghton persuaded me to take a leave of absence from Springfield College, and from 1993 to 1996, I led a fledgling technology business for the company, getting something like a hands-on MBA in the process.

As I prepared to return to Springfield College, I was nominated for the presidency of tiny Marlboro College, located in the hills of southern Vermont. Being only thirty-seven years old, I was sure I had no shot at the job but thought interviewing would be a good learning experience. I arrived for the interview in the late afternoon, and knowing that energies would be flagging for the search committee members by then, I brought warm cookies. The chair of the board, Lil Farber, later told me that while I was not yet their choice, the cookies ensured I'd make it to the next round.

I was eventually offered the job, so in 1996, my wife, Pat, and I moved to that bucolic campus with Emma and Hannah, our eight- and six-year-old daughters. I served there for seven years, learned an enormous amount, and accomplished a lot. We revitalized a tired physical plant, raised tens of millions of dollars, elevated the college's profile, and located much-needed new sources of revenue. Despite all of that, I was never able to persuade the college community to grow or pursue new online programs that could have solved the structural limitations of Marlboro's size, which would eventually catch up with it and lead to its closure in 2020. Worse, I was never a really great cultural fit. For all that was going so well, I was ready to leave in 2003, and I think most of the campus community was ready to say goodbye to me.

So in 2003, I arrived at Southern New Hampshire University (SNHU). At the time it had about 2,500 students, mostly in its residential campus program, a $50 million budget, little endowment or reserves, a worn-out campus, and scant brand awareness. But its mission was focused on students, and it had a hunger to grow and improve, some history of innovation, and a small online program. My gracious predecessor, Dick Gustafson, had brought the place back from the brink of closure during his sixteen years there, started the online program, and stabilized the finances. In a story that has been told in many other places, we embraced online learning and transformed SNHU into the country's largest university, serving one hundred eighty thousand learners at the time of this writing.

Along the way, we rebuilt the outdated campus, hired thousands of people across the country, innovated around new program design and technology, surpassed the $1 billion mark, and made SNHU one of the best-known universities in the country. With a relentless focus on underserved learners, we have more people of color enrolled with us than do the largest historically Black colleges and universities. We bring full-degree programs to refugees in places like Lebanon, Kenya, and South Africa, and we serve homeless kids and deferred action for childhood arrivals (DACA) students. We use our resources to feed low-income kids in our home city of Manchester, created the Center for New Americans, invest in Black-owned and -managed equity funds, support military families, and more. We also treat our people well, being the sole university named to the *Chronicle of Higher Education*'s Great Colleges to Work For list every year since its inception.

No longer that wet-behind-the-ears new president who arrived in southern Vermont, I have been honored to serve in a variety of leadership roles in American higher education. I have chaired the American Council on Education board and the Association of Governing Boards' Council of Presidents. I have served on the National Academies board on Higher Education and Workforce, as well as the boards of the Council of Independent Colleges, the Council for Adult and Experiential Learning, the Visiting Committee for Harvard's Graduate School of Education, and our regional commission on higher education. US Senator Patty Murray of Washington nominated me to the National Advisory Committee on Institutional Quality and Integrity, the quasi-government committee that advises the US secretary of education on matters of accreditation—sort of the accreditor of accreditors.

In 2018, I received the Teachers Insurance and Annuity Association's Theodore M. Hesburgh Award for Leadership Excellence, named for the legendary president of the University of Notre Dame. Previous winners included Brit Kirwan, Freeman Hrabowski, and Gail Mellow—presidents I place on a pedestal. To be included in their number was incredibly moving, an honor I was not sure I deserved. A first-generation college graduate, a working-class kid without a blue chip pedigree, I stood in front of the ballroom with a healthy sense of impostor syndrome, wishing my parents were still alive to be there.

The professional journey I've just outlined will provide what is needed to follow the stories I share in the chapters that follow. For my personal journey, I offer this next account.

My Story: The Personal Journey

My family immigrated to the Boston area from Gaytons, a hardscrabble Acadian farming community in New Brunswick, Canada. It was a place where the men went away to find work, sometimes for weeks and often months, leaving their wives behind to tend to small farms, take care of children, and get by in a place that was late getting paved roads, indoor plumbing, and adequate medical care. The poorest part of Canada, Gaytons was what some called French Appalachia.

My parents had eighth-grade educations, five kids to feed, and not nearly enough money. So they sold what little they had and joined relatives who had immigrated to the Boston area for work and better lives. That meant living with those relatives at first and then in a rented apartment in a multiunit building in Waltham's poorest neighborhood, where Irish and Italians had lived before us, and Puerto Ricans and

Dominicans had followed. My mother got a job in a factory, my father as a laborer, and we started our version of the American Dream.

By the time I reached first grade, I could read well, but my spoken English still sounded funny, and other kids would make fun of me. My teacher, Mrs. McKenna, would routinely ask me to read aloud in front of the class, which was so humiliating that I once avoided going to school by hiding behind the service station dumpster next door to my apartment. It was a deeply flawed plan. I had a six-year-old's sense of time. Within twenty minutes, I got bored and ate my lunch. In another thirty minutes or so, I showed up at my door thinking that the day had surely passed by then. My mother, surprised, asked why I was home after only an hour, what had happened to my lunch, and how my clothes had gotten so dirty. Subsequent variations on my strategy to avoid reading in front of the class worked no better, and when I finally divulged why I didn't want to go to school, my mother met with the school principal—the wonderfully named Mr. Sentence—who spoke to me, then to Mrs. McKenna. I was never again subjected to the embarrassment of reading aloud in class, and Mrs. McKenna never warmed up to me after that incident.

I had no interest in the odd version of French spoken by my Acadian family. An immigrant kid's desire to shed his language and fit in is familiar to any nonnative child. Also common to many immigrant children is the lack of interest in one's cultural roots, which often feel more like a burden until after childhood, when one starts thinking about self-identity. At that point, a culture so long ignored and even resisted becomes a source of differentiation, identity, and insight. Before then, in an effort to escape that reality, one's history is at risk of being self-erased as well. It would be years before I would start to reclaim that knowledge.

It started for me when my wife, Pat, and I were dating, and I took her to Gaytons to see where I was from and meet family. We sat in kitchens warmed by wood ovens still used for cooking (and this was 1978!), found my father's rough wood desk from his childhood in an uncle's attic, and visited the old farmhouse my family had sold when we left Canada. My cousin, one of thirteen children, recalled being so poor that when my Aunt Celia had to go into town in winter to buy supplies, one of the older kids would have to stay home from school so Celia could use her boots. If New Brunswick is Canada's poorest province, Acadians were its least educated, poorest, and most rural citizens. Going back to it as a college student, I could see the poverty in ways I hadn't recognized in visits as a child, when outhouses and horse-pulled hay wagons seemed more exotic than a reflection of deprivation.

Pat asked lots of questions, and I could not answer many of them. The act of bringing in someone from the outside, struggling to explain my own culture, is a little painful. What I realized was how little I actually understood it. I was like a goldfish who no longer noticed it was in water until someone asked about it. During that visit, Pat and I sat on a blanket on the earthen rampart of nearby Fort Beauséjour—the French fort that protected Acadia from the British and succumbed to Boston-based American provincial troops in 1755—reading a history I did not know. My cultural history.

History's losers rarely recover. Generational poverty has persisted among Acadians, who would never catch up with English-speaking Protestants. The Acadians had fallen too far behind in terms of land, wealth accumulation, access to credit, and education. While visiting relatives there even in the 1960s, I remember using a chamber pot on nights that were too cold to visit the outhouse, and using an outside pump when fetching water for my aunt. My mother recalled a childhood memory of following a priest eating an orange and eagerly picking up the rinds he carelessly tossed aside so she could suck on the pith.

Protestants went to provincial schools, while my family members went to those run by the Catholic Church. The church led the cultural renaissance of Acadians, ran schools and charities, and was a source of comfort for many. But my family also tells of domineering and often imperious village priests who dictated much of day-to-day life.

There is a delicious irony in our older daughter, Emma, moving in 2014 to Kedgwick, New Brunswick, an Acadian community of impoverished forest workers living on the fringes of capitalism and finding ways to subvert and resist another colonizer, this time Irving Oil instead of the British. Emma was visiting my sister in New Brunswick while home from Oxford, where she was studying anthropology with a special interest in communities that create their own informal systems of law, commerce, and being. Originally planning to do her research in Syria with nomadic tribes, she was ordered out by Syrian officials during the growing civil war. In New Brunswick, she stumbled upon another such community—Acadians in the remote northern forests. Emma spent almost two years there doing fieldwork as she completed her doctorate.

I eventually sent her dissertation to my siblings, and they were fascinated. Like the goldfish, they and I were in many ways understanding our culture for the first time. What we saw in her dissertation was our culture at its best and worst. I recognized my extended family on every page. The love of being in the woods, of hunting and fishing, of music and alcohol and raucous parties late into the night, of trucks and machines, of work that breaks a body, of spending all you have today and sharing with others. There is also the coarseness, the lack of education, the disorderliness of lives spent on the economic margins.

Early while getting reacquainted with Acadian culture, I found myself in central Louisiana doing consulting work at LSU of Alexandria. That Saturday, I rented a car and drove into Cajun country. I had a beer at Fred's Lounge in Mamou (self-billed as the Cajun Music Capital of the World), listened to zydeco, and was surrounded by Bouchers, Boudreaus, and LeBlancs, and they all looked like my relatives. That evening over dinner with friends in Alexandria, I was waxing on about these long-lost cousins, when my friend Stacy only half-joked, "Well, y'all know that around here Cajuns are sort of known for skirting the law, sleeping around, and drinking too much and driving off bridges."

Even though I had reveled in the warmth of the companionship, the infectious music, and the sense of familial familiarity among my Cajun cousins, I also recognized the fallen-down buildings, the junk in the yards, and the rough-looking men and women clustered around pickup tailgates with beers and cigarettes. It all felt like home, good and bad.

Acadians are underdogs, so they immediately feel great kinship with other downtrodden people. From Emma's dissertation:

> Acadians are seen as the losers of history and capitalism, and insider values are construed fundamentally as subaltern values. People regularly draw explicit connections between local Kedgwick insiders and other peoples perceived to belong to the same moral community through their shared subalternity. Acadianité, or Acadianness, may be most clearly demonstrated by speaking French and having the right name and ancestry (Keppie 2013:318), but Acadian is also a relative status. Acadians are defined as the downtrodden, and the insider sphere is often extended to anyone in an "Acadian" position, from Syrian refugees to Amazonian tribes exploited by multinational companies or even deer, birds, and fish whose habitat is threatened. On Facebook, for example, people in Kedgwick post links to articles about indigenous struggles over natural resources in Latin America and Papua New Guinea, emphasizing the similarity of their values and their exploitation.

When people from Kedgwick go on vacation in Cuba, they often befriend the staff at the hotels where they stay and end up incorporating them into their networks of resource-sharing, sending them money, clothes, shoes, towels, and school supplies once they return to Canada. When people in Kedgwick found out that New Brunswick was going to accept Syrian refugees, they began collecting goods for them, from winter clothes to canned food. One local woman even insisted that she wanted to donate her car. The downtrodden are seen as fellow moral insiders, both because their enemies—the corporations, governments, and militaries responsible for their oppression—are seen as prototypical outsiders, greedy, self-interested, and obsessed with profit, and because the Kedgwiquois recognize the link between insider moral principles and poverty and political marginalization.[4]

My father liked to watch the news and follow politics, and he always rooted for the underdog. He was the only person I knew who wanted the Argentinians to prevail in the Falklands War (his long-standing antipathy to the British no doubt contributed to that sentiment). My mother rushed to help anyone in need, welcomed people of all races and backgrounds into her kitchen, and had a rare ability to forgive almost any wrong.

There are many stories of my parents' generosity. For example, in the gossipy ways of small farming villages, a local woman who was marginally better off than my mother frequently badmouthed her. Yet when her panicked husband knocked on the door at 2 AM asking for help because she was having a difficult delivery, my mother bundled up and assisted in the birth. When the woman woke up the next morning, it was my mother who was rocking the swaddled newborn while keeping a watchful eye on the woman. I used to think it was because she was

Catholic and had some innate understanding of redemption or forgiveness, but I think it was because she was Acadian. Or perhaps both.

My parents' ethos also included tolerance. On a Christmas Eve, my family had stopped at the local general store to buy something, and my father gave his last dollar to someone out front panhandling—a guy in the village who everyone knew had a drinking problem. When my mother mentioned that he would probably just spend the money on drink, my father's reply was, "If that's the best Christmas he can have, I'm glad I can help."

Similarly, I had a cousin who routinely got into trouble with the law. People would hide their wallets when he was in their house, and he was the subject of constant criticism for being a bad kid. But my parents welcomed him in, fed him, and reminded people of the rough childhood he had suffered. When a judge eventually gave him a choice between prison and Vietnam, his letters home from those faraway jungles were to my parents.

An extension of that underdog mentality and the "there but for the grace of God go I" sympathy that runs through Acadian culture and my family's is an assessment of people on their basic human traits: kindness, generosity, parenting style, loyalty, and work ethic (to be lazy in my family was just about the worst thing possible). When I became a college president, I often invited my mother to events where she got to meet some pretty famous people. She once sat next to then-Kenyan vice president Moody Awori. They ignored the room, chatting about their grandchildren, growing up poor, and their Catholic faith. She didn't know he was a wealthy and powerful politician, but she did remark on what a good man he seemed to be. Likewise, he said he most enjoyed the conversation with her that evening. Notably, my mother also spent as much time in avid conversation with the dining service team working the event at our home that night, no less interested in them than she was in a world leader.

On another occasion, when she was eighty-two, I obtained a passport for her and brought her to London—her first trip abroad and maybe only her second plane ride. While there, I received a call that Emmylou Harris was in the city and wanted to invite me to tea at her hotel (she was a supporter of Marlboro College, where I was president). I sheepishly asked if I could bring my mother along. Though I explained that Emmylou was a famous musician, my mother seemed to miss that key point, and when she sat down, smiled, and said, "So, Emmylou, you're a musician. Do you teach music?" Emmylou smiled and graciously explained that she was a performer. My mother wanted to know all about that, if she had played growing up, what her parents did, and more. Aside from occasionally turning to me to say how much she loved my mother and that she reminded her so much of her own grandmother, Emmylou pretty much forgot I was there.

When Emmylou's road manager, a burly guy with forearms bigger than my waist and a rat-tail beard, came in to say they would have to leave soon for a sound check, Emmylou introduced him. My mother shook his hand, smiled, and asked him if he, too, was a musician. Within minutes he had pulled up a chair, poured a cup of tea, and they chatted away, the three of them. My mother connected with everyone as a human being and cared little for what they did and what they earned.

In fact, in Acadian culture, what one did for work, how much they earned, and attaining success in either would more likely be suspect than envied. In her dissertation, Emma describes Acadian values as egalitarian, communal, and tolerant. An extension of those values is a distrust of wealth and power. In my extended family, those who were doing better—measured by living in a nicer house, moving to a better town, or driving a fancier car (or, just as often, truck)—were admired but also a little suspect. Suspect of what? It's not clear, but some combination of selfishness if they did not humbly share their wealth (but doing so in a gracious way, not to show off) and thinking themselves better than others and less a part of the clan.

Any claim to superiority or putting on airs is disdained. My mother had for years mentioned that someday she would have a fur coat, so we bought her one when she was in her sixties. But my father was so appalled at the idea of people thinking she was showing off that I cannot recall a single instance when she wore that coveted coat in public. And when I went off to college, I acquired the family nickname the Professor from my brother-in-law, which was mostly said out of respect for my bookishness but also carried a hint of skepticism, since bookishness is implicitly linked to ineptitude with tools and machines, and an aversion to hard work—the worst thing of all.

The relationship of Acadian sensibilities and values to working-class consciousness is a bit complicated. We were undoubtedly working class, but there are working-class cultures that do not eye financial success with suspicion, resent those who move into wealthier neighborhoods, or place greater value on education than staying in place. I hesitate to make generalizations for groups not my own, but I think of working-class immigrant cultures from Southeast Asia and South Asia in contrast to Acadians, where the former cultures celebrate professional and material success without a sense of betrayal. They believe in capitalism and its systems and readily embrace its rewards.

Acadians historically have denied the opportunities of the system even as they were exploited on its behalf. They see material success as some kind of violation of cultural values, implicitly asking, "Were you egalitarian enough? Did you take care of the larger group?" Acadians are more likely to "work the system," knowing that it is rigged against them anyway. In Kedgwick, that often means a side hustle growing and selling marijuana, working just enough weeks to still get unemployment benefits, or embracing the local biker gang that protects the drug transport routes along remote logging roads because they are Acadian, loyal, and quick to help out in ways not associated with the police, who tread wearily in such a community. It's not that Acadians don't work hard; it's that they work hard outside of (and often against) a system that never accepted them, that shows them little care, that grinds them down in the backbreaking work of extraction industries like forestry, which offers too little of everything else such as quality medical care and education. They prefer to work for themselves and on their own.

In my own family, even after immigration, no one worked for large employers. Most preferred their independence and worked for themselves, often in the trades, and did not join unions. Women, like my mother, worked for small employers in retail or manufacturing. Most did not like being told what to do. My favorite uncle, Wilfred, was once working on a hot day under a blazing sun, pouring concrete walkways in a new apartment complex. The general contractor walked up and said, "Wilfred, can't you go any faster?" Wilfred took out the cigarette that always dangled from the corner of his mouth, stood up, and said, "Yep, I can go faster," and walked over to his truck and drove away. That story has been told and retold in my family, not only for the knowing smiles it elicits (Wilfred was a character, even in a family of characters), but because it captures an admirable Acadian orneriness and a small act of dignified rebellion that family members admire. So Acadians are certainly working class and, if not proudly so, culturally disposed to resist the systems that promise class mobility. They are modest in their aspirations and suspicious of what it takes to attain success as commonly defined.

South Side Waltham, anchored by the Waltham Watch Factory, was a working-class neighborhood of densely packed multifamily buildings and is where I mostly grew up. The backyards abutted, and the men would water their gardens after work, leaning on the chain-link fences that separated the yards, smoking cigarettes, and talking. There was Mr. Pappas, a Greek American and a police officer. And Al, an Italian American and a carpet guy. And Tony, a Portuguese American and a trades-man. Childhood games might range across multiple yards, and anyone's mother had license to give you a cuff on the side of the head if you mis-behaved. When, as adolescents, we left the South Side to go to Waltham's one high school, we became much more aware of our class status as we met kids from the city's nicer neighborhoods. They lived in single-family homes, drove nicer cars, dated each other for the most part, and always seemed better looking—with straight teeth (no one I knew had braces) and good hair. They later attended schools like Harvard, Bowdoin, and Holy Cross, while the smaller number of us who went to college attended more affordable and less selective state colleges (you could at the time apply to any three for something like one hundred dollars).

It was only in my senior year, when I had made friends with some of those other kids, that I realized the difference for them was not just the material things that I mostly envied. I can remember using roofing tin and pipe clamps to patch a hole in the exhaust system of my old Impala, while they drove muscle cars like 442s and Camaros. Better wheels aside, they moved through the world differently. They were confident, they felt like they belonged and knew good things would come to them. In contrast, when I hung out with them, I felt very much on the edge of the circle, uncertain about everything (what to wear, what to say, how to act), and more acutely conscious of what was different in my family.

I later sought to understand the implication of my social class by joining a Marxist study group in college and later doing doctoral-level research on working-class agitation in nineteenth-century British fiction. I came to wear my working-class roots with pride. It was a painful transition, sometimes fueled by resentment and characterized by ambivalence. Because even when I came to own my working-class background and associate it with values that I still hold dear—my parents' generosity and tolerance, work ethic, common sense, and sense of community—exposure to middle- and upper-class life made me increasingly cringe at the coarseness, lack of refinement, and limited worldview of my social class.

By the time I got to graduate school, I knew people who vacationed in places I had only read about in books and magazines, while I inevitably drove back to Gaytons to see relatives without actually using the word *vacation*. I was being exposed to ethnic cuisines, while the most daring we ever got was Italian takeout from the Château Restaurant.

My head was exploding with new ideas, theories, and disciplines that no one was interested in discussing when I went home. Then I met Pat, whose family was as down to earth as mine but was solidly middle class, living in a single-family home with a family business in construction and a lumberyard, and taking actual vacations on Cape Cod. She was a feminist, listened to cooler music, rejected Catholicism, read feminist writer Shulamith Firestone and Karl Marx (she was one reason I joined that study group), watched foreign films, and was like no woman I knew in Waltham. She adored my family and embraced them for who they were. Falling in love with her was a more important step in class mobility than money or possessions. She modeled and then changed the way I would be in the world.

Like so many tweeners, I came to inhabit the middle ground between a social class full of people I loved and who loved me—the source of my core values, the comfort of home—and a social class that fed my imagination and intellect, that promised a bigger world, that held the material satisfactions of professional success. The former felt insufficient and in the latter I felt an impostor, thus my ambivalence to both. I have had countless conversations with other academics who share my story of class mobility, and they describe the tweener dynamic, sometimes quite emotionally. In the end, because my values are so grounded in my working-class life, I feel most at home there. Our best friends, even those far more successful and wealthier than we are, share those roots.

In my imagined Venn diagram that captures the intersection of Acadian culture and working-class life, the third prominent circle is Catholicism. The church dominated village life for Acadians, was a large part of Acadian resistance to British (and thus Anglican) rule, and remained a large part of my upbringing after we immigrated. That included regular Sunday mass, first communion and confirmation, Sunday school, and occasional youth activities at Saint Charles Catholic Church, where we attended.

Pat is Irish American, and her Catholic upbringing included parochial school, severe nuns using corporal punishment, and fearful invocations of hell and death that led her to run from Catholicism and religion in general. My memories are a stark contrast. Sunday mass was always followed by a wonderful breakfast of bacon and eggs and toasted homemade bread with jam that my mother had made.

Father Jim McDonald was our parish priest and while not French, he had been a hockey player at Saint Michael's College and thus enjoyed honorary status. He taught me and others how to skate and later coached our youth hockey team. I liked helping out at the rectory, the crisp cleanliness of the vestments, the smell of incense at mass, the small boxes of milk and commercially made Peggy Lawton Choco-Chip Cookies served at Sunday school (since we had to fast before taking communion, I was always starving by then). Later, as teenagers, we knew to go to Saturday's 7 PM mass if the Bruins were playing because Father McDonald would speed things along so as not to miss the opening face-off. I often went to sleep hearing my mother whispering her rosary in the adjacent room. It was a comforting sound to me.

While a lapsed Catholic, I am at home in churches, and attending a mass (usually a wedding or a funeral these days) is like donning a comfortable pair of old slippers I haven't worn in a while. The Catholics I grew up with do not share any real level of biblical familiarity in the way that so many Protestants do. Their relationship with God is mediated through a church hierarchy that is often heavy-handed. My father, good Acadian that he was, had little use for priests telling him how to live, and the church sex abuse scandals almost drove my mother away, furious as she was with the awfulness of the acts and outraged at the hypocrisy of men who otherwise felt just fine policing the moral behavior of rural village life. Despite all that is wrong with the Catholic Church, and that's a fair bit, I felt comfortable in it and continue to believe that if we all genuinely followed Jesus's teaching, the world would be a kinder, more compassionate, more equitable place.

My most important learning from my Catholic upbringing and the part I carry with me to this day is a sense of complicity, that our decisions have a moral dimension. In some ways, complicity is the positive flip side of the Catholic guilt that Pat and I still joke about—the idea that my decisions and, more importantly, my failings, are tied to the idea of connectedness, community, and responsibility for and to others. They have ethical and moral consequences. That means not making decisions only in the moment or for oneself but thinking more broadly. The decisions we make as consumers—the sourcing of our coffee, the mileage of our new car, the manufacturing ethics of that shirt we covet—make us complicit in the good and the bad consequences of those decisions.

In graduate school, I became quite taken with the work of American novelist William Dean Howells, whose work deals with social class,

class mobility, and this idea of complicity. According to Howells scholars Clara and Rudolph Kirk, Howells's understanding of complicity "means that all lives are involved with all others, the sum total of which is God."[5] That sense of connectedness, when the universe feels fully aligned, can reach near metaphysical levels, as when Pat kissed me for the first time (I felt like Levin in *Anna Karenina* after the board game, when he realizes Kitty will marry him), the moment I first laid eyes on our two babies entering the world, when my parents died, and a handful of other events. However, it infuses my day-to-day life in a way that I rarely reveal. I've had people say I seem largely unflappable, but they do not know how I worry about almost everything. I think it's my Catholic self at work, and I prize it because it says that things matter, that others matter, and that I owe them, in the best sense of that debt, the debt of our common humanity.

My Acadian sense of community and connection to underdogs, my working-class sensibility and values, and my Catholic sense of moral complicity and responsibility define the moral space I inhabit as a person and a leader. It is why I love my university. I often describe SNHU as a blue-collar institution, one that is deeply grounded in a mission of transforming the lives of students who I think of as underdogs—the nearly 40 percent of Americans who say they would struggle to come up with four hundred dollars for an unexpected car repair.[6]

Our faculty and staff embrace that mission and are devoted to our students and their success. We do not chase status or the signals of institutional superiority—no Division 1 sports, no research function, no big-name faculty, no signature buildings designed by famous architects. We stay laser focused on students, taking good care of our own, and we say in our mission statement that we will "relentlessly challenge the status quo." Danielle Stanton, our vice president of human resources, teases me because on my Caliper personality assessment, I barely even registered on the "works well within frameworks of authority" item.

We are routinely ranked one of the country's most innovative institutions because we rarely accept the "this is the way it has always been done" constraints that infuse higher education. We chafe when told we can't do something, a very Acadian reaction. SNHU feels like home to me, and while I have never loved any institution, I love this one and will finish my career here (as long as the trustees will have me), because at a time of growing inequity and lack of social mobility, when higher education is increasingly seen as part of the problem, out of reach for too many, burdening graduates with debilitating debt, and seeing too many students drop out, SNHU seeks to be part of the solution.

I have long taken it for granted that organizations assume the values of those who lead them. Even in smaller units within an organization, people will come to mimic the ways of their manager, responding to what is rewarded and what is punished, what is measured and what is valued. Long before I arrived, SNHU was focused on students, was down to earth in its culture, generous in its aid to students in financial need. I can take no credit for those qualities, but they resonated with me. Perhaps in a symbiotic way, I came to amplify and build on those core qualities even as SNHU and the work we do reaffirmed and strengthened those core values and sensibilities I associate with my culture, my upbringing, my class, and my religion.

I was recently courted for the presidency of a flagship public university, a Research 1–designated institution with a well-known Division I football team that often plays on national television, an esteemed medical school, world-class researchers, a gorgeous campus in an attractive city, and enviable metrics in terms of selectivity, levels of state support, national and international reach, and more. I thanked the search firm representative who called, and I graciously declined. The trustee heading the search committee then called, and I again said I was very flattered, but I was happy at SNHU. She found out I was to be in a meeting in her city and camped out in the waiting area. When she saw me, she made her best pitch, offering what was, for almost anyone, a dream job. But not for me. In that moment, when I felt no spark and she had little response to my questions about the low number of low-income students served, the low number of in-state students enrolled, the low graduation rate for students of color, and the bold ideas they had for the future, I knew that I was already in the right job. At least for how I have come to measure success and what matters to me.

In the course of my career, I have done an enormous amount of writing and presenting—from books and blogs to essays, columns, and conference keynote addresses. The topics have ranged from innovation to accreditation to leadership and others. Rarely have I written about my values, at least explicitly, and even less often have I written about concepts like grace, mattering, aspiration, and storytelling. Neglecting these concepts when trying to reform human-focused systems is like trying to address climate change without addressing the fundamental ways in which we choose to live. All the technology, cap and trade, and international agreements will not save the planet if we don't also rethink our attitudes toward consumption, material goods, stewardship of natural resources, and capitalism—in sum, we need to rethink our values as well as come up with concrete solutions.

Likewise, we cannot make critical societal systems such as criminal justice, health care, and education human-centered if we do not address fundamental human values. I am embarrassed that in a career as long as mine, I have rarely foregrounded the most important questions—the ones that have to do with seeing people for who they are, the power of forgiveness and redemption, helping others dream bigger dreams for themselves, the gravitational pull of narrative, and the love for those we serve. I like to think those values have informed my work along the way, so rooted are they in my upbringing. In the chapters that follow, I explore those concepts, share the stories of others, recall my own stories, and invite you to connect it all to the way you work within systems, how you lead, and *your* story, the story that matters most in the end.

Deaths of despair, civil unrest, political schisms, and loneliness amid hyper-connectedness in modern American life have their roots in humanity denied, the anger and resignation of people who feel as though they do not matter to the world or the systems meant to serve them. This exploration includes stories of people working to rehumanize the systems and organizations in which they work and lead. They are taking ideas like mattering and aspiration and translating them into action, providing alternatives and better solutions for the people they seek to serve. They provide inspiration and models for how we can get it right.

When systems fail the people they are meant to serve, it's almost always because of a failure of human values more than any inherent attribute of the system. Almost always someone made a choice. So, too, the inverse. If systems are to better serve the people for whom they are intended, their success will start not with the rational design of policies and technologies and processes—as important as it is to get those right—but with the design of the heart. In every conference room in every building at SNHU is a sign that reads, "Are the decisions we made here today good for students?" Not good for us. Not good for the system in which we work. But good for the human beings for whom we exist.

MATTERING

oston's Brigham and Women's Hospital is one of the finest hospitals in the world. In 2015, my mother-in-law, Rosella, lay unconscious and dying in one of its rooms, connected to tubes and monitors, receiving treatments that were fending off the inevitable for just a bit longer. As the days dragged on, the toll on the family grew. Christine, one of the more senior nurses on the floor, took it all in during her routine checks and finally asked Fred, my father-in-law, "Is this working for Rosella? Would she be OK with this if she could tell us?" When he quietly, but unequivocally, said no, she replied, "I think it's time to bring the boys in."

The boys were the amazing doctors—world-class in their specialties—keeping Rosella alive. The next day, they assembled with the family in Rosella's room, and Christine methodically went from one doctor to the other asking for a status report. She listened patiently, taking notes, as the endocrinologist read off data points, talked about frequency of dialysis and how her kidney functions were stable. The cardiologist did the same, and so on. When they finished,

Christine looked up from her notes, turned her gaze to Rosella, then asked them, "Doctors, how is this going to play out for Rosella?" They all looked at their shoes, hesitant to say aloud what everyone in the room knew. Christine then asked my wife's family if it was "time to let Rosella go." They unhesitatingly assented, eager to end this torture of her limbo state.

Christine thanked the doctors for their care and asked everyone to leave the room for thirty minutes. When the family returned, the tubes and monitors were gone, Rosella's hair neatly brushed. In the new-found quiet, absent the beeps and whirs of medical equipment, Rosella entered her last hours with restored dignity and peace for a humane passing from this world.

Brigham and Women's offers best-in-class medical treatment, employs some of the finest medical professionals in the world, and is exactly the place I want to go if I ever have a serious ailment. Yet even in its excellence, it is a hospital within a system of hospitals within an American health-care system that in that moment lost sight of an essential human need it was not addressing or even recognizing. It took Christine, a frontline worker in touch daily with the actual person at the heart of this small drama, to remind everyone that Rosella mattered—not the tests, protocols, or procedures available to her doctors. Indeed, the very things the system was designed to offer had come to dehumanize Rosella, to make her matter less than the system that was there to serve her, and to earn the growing resentment of family seeing someone they loved lost in a health-care machine that was making more money the longer the ordeal persisted. It took Christine to remind everyone that the person the system was serving mattered most, to *see* Rosella again, and to rehumanize its care of her.

Christine reminded the system that Rosella mattered.

Mattering goes to the fundamental human need to be seen, to know that it is important to the world and others that you are here. It speaks to the very core of human fulfillment—not happiness, but satisfaction. Mattering plays out in our day-to-day lives in circumstances like marriages, family dynamics (ask any middle child), friendships, and team sports. When someone remembers your birthday, calls to check in, or does a favor without asking, you realize you matter to them, and it touches your heart.

Mattering also plays out in our everyday encounters with systems. I know Amica Insurance might not be the least expensive option for me, but in every encounter I've had, its employees made me feel like I matter to the company and to the person on the other end of the call. Dr. Bill Holgerson, our family physician, is routinely named one of the best doctors in Boston, partly because of great customer service: we are never kept waiting (though he has excellent magazines in the waiting room), his staff is both warm and efficient, and the patient portal he uses gives us immediate access to test results, his notes, and more. But the real reason he is so good is that he takes time to listen, to know us, and to talk.

There is a large body of research that shows that doctors who simply spend more time talking to their patients are sued for malpractice at significantly lower rates—even when they make mistakes.[1] I don't know if Bill is more skilled as a physician, but I do know he is exceptional in making his patients feel like they matter. And that may be the best medicine.

We live our lives within systems that ostensibly exist to serve us, to provide care, protection, and basic needs. Public education, health care, social assistance, and the criminal justice systems ostensibly exist to improve people's lives, yet they routinely fail them. In fact, they often dehumanize the very people they are meant to serve, making them feel like they do not matter. If a little boy wakes up every morning in a house without heat and no adult bothering to make breakfast for him, see him off to school, or greet him when he returns, he won't feel like he matters very much to his family. If his classrooms contain few supplies, have outdated books, lack adequate heat in winter, and have so many students that his teachers barely know his name, he won't feel like he matters much to his school. If his walk back home is through dirty, littered streets that are often unsafe, he won't feel like he matters much to his city. Is it any surprise, then, that such a boy would later join a gang that not only wants him and will protect him, but has expectations of him as well? When his whole world communicates that it does not matter if he is hungry, learning, safe, or even alive, a gang that says he matters—that tells him that he has value—is a powerful lure.

Social scientists have taken up the topic of mattering, and there are few more expert than Greg Elliott, a Brown University sociologist who has conducted extensive research on mattering's motivational impact on behavior and from whom I borrow the term. In a 2009 article in the *Journal of Family Issues*, Greg explains that mattering has three facets: awareness, importance, and reliance.[2] Do others know you exist? Do they invest time and resources in you? Do they look to you as a resource? Greg believes this is the fundamental motivation of all humans. "Above else, there's a need to matter," he explained to me. To be clear, there is in mattering a need to be recognized as an individual, as a person who has value. But mattering also includes feeling part of something bigger than ourselves. As Greg told me,

> we need to have a sense that we are part of a recognized group, what Émile Durkheim calls the importance of solidarity. That does two things. First, it integrates you so that you are a member of something that's much bigger than yourself. Second, it acts as an

agent of social control, because if you are truly committed to the group, you will have an internalized incentive to make sure you don't do anything to damage the group. You will self-regulate.

Mattering is not mere belonging. If I join a professional association, I can pay my dues, receive its publications, attend its conferences, and value the benefits offered to me but not feel like I matter to the organization. A job can feel this way if the employer makes me feel like I do not exist, doesn't invest in me, or doesn't treat me as a resource—which is how much of America's labor force feels. I might argue that the pandemic more fully surfaced that sense. The result is people refusing to go back to positions in which they feel they do not matter, as evidenced by their pay, hours, and working conditions. The result is ten million unfilled jobs at the time of this writing and a labor supply crisis across many industry sectors.[3]

Not mattering can lead to dissatisfaction at work, at home, or with a vendor. When it permeates one's life, it more powerfully leads to shame and a loss of dignity and self-respect. James Gilligan, who worked in prisons and directed Harvard University's Center for the Study of Violence, argues that shame is the source of most violent behavior. In his superb 1996 book *Violence*, he writes:

> The prison inmates I work with have told me repeatedly, when I asked them why they had assaulted someone, that it was because "he disrespected me," or "he disrespected my visit" (meaning "visitor"). The word is so central in the vocabulary, moral value system, and psychodynamics of these chronically violent men that they have abbreviated it into the slang term, "he dis'ed me."[4]

Gilligan cites the anthropologist Julian Pitt-Rivers, who observed that in all cultures the "withdrawal of respect" induces shame. When we feel we do not matter, when we are not worthy of respect or even notice, or when our humanity is actively stripped away from us, we are shamed. As Gilligan asserts, "For men who have lived for a lifetime on a diet of contempt and disdain, the temptation to gain instant respect in this way can be worth far more than the cost of going to prison, or even dying."[5] He concludes that "the emotion of shame is the primary or ultimate cause of all violence."[6]

On this question of violence and mattering, I often recall our daughter Emma returning from time in a West Bank refugee camp and saying that she understood suicide bombers for the first time. As she explained, she had met young Palestinian men with no prospect of a job and thus little prospect of marriage and children. Subjected to the daily humiliation of checkpoint inspections and arbitrary detainment and violence, they were told they had no value and were unable to imagine a better life, unable to see any viable path for that life even if they could imagine it. Their day-to-day existence taught them in visceral ways that they do not matter. In an honor culture such as theirs, they only knew daily shame. Then a jihadi recruiter tells them they can play a role in striking back at their oppressor, to be a hero, to be celebrated on posters on camp walls, and to be rewarded in the next life as a martyr—to finally *matter*, albeit through gruesome violence. Emma said the psychology of the suicide bomber made sense to her for the first time. When I shared that story with Greg, he replied:

That's what Seung-Hui Cho, who shot up Virginia Tech in 2007, put in his manifesto. "They didn't know me. They're going to be sorry they ignored me." He knew he was going to die, and he was OK with that because at least he would die having made a difference, in his mind. People would know he existed. Or as the old adage goes, "I'd rather be hated than ignored."

While the violence of a campus shooter or a criminal reflects the acts of an individual, the sense that one does not matter—and the loss of dignity and shame that comes with that feeling—can coalesce into a social movement or civil unrest. The protests and sometimes violence and looting in American streets in the summer of 2020 are well explained in Frantz Fanon's 1961 book *The Wretched of the Earth*, and dramatically captured in Richard Wright's *Native Son*, two books that have stayed with me since college. Both explain violence as an assertion of one's humanity when that humanity is denied at every turn, when hope for a better life is nowhere to be found. In Fanon's analysis, it is in the violence of the struggle against colonialism that identity is formed and through which a people can shape their mattering (though he doesn't use that word). He writes that "hunger with dignity is preferable to bread eaten in slavery."[7]

Establishment America condemns the destruction we saw in cities in the summer of 2020, asserting that basic rules of respect for property must be observed. However, when people of color do obey the rules of our game—work really hard, take care of their families, educate themselves—they are still shut out of the rewards. A traffic stop is still a life-threatening danger. Career advancement is still limited. That college degree will cost them more and earn them less than it does their White classmates.

Those are objective facts. Don't play by the rules, and White America will jail you, shoot you, and demonize you. White America may very well do that even if you *do* play by its rules. In either case, the social contract does not extend to you, but still we want you to agree to your end of it, the work hard and don't misbehave part, even as we ignore our end, the promise of fair opportunity and a better life for you and your kids. Greg says it's "like the football player who gets tackled by a player running off the bench. That's not fair. I don't get frustrated if the opposing defensive linebacker tackles me. That's his job. But if you come running off the bench and keep me from scoring a touchdown . . . wait a minute."

White society does not extend the social contract to Black America, and when people of color insist on their mattering, sometimes using violence when nothing else is left to them, we invoke the rules of a rigged game in which they are denied their fair opportunity and basic respect. As Fanon might ask, "Why are you surprised that someone then ignores your rules and burns down a Target store?" Deny too long the existence and mattering of a people, and they will assert their humanity in ways that get society's attention. If you deprive them of a place in the game, don't be surprised if they then refuse to play by the rules of the game from which they are excluded.

A parallel might be found in the violent storming of the Capitol Building in Washington, DC, by Trump supporters and White nationalist groups like the Proud Boys and NSC-131 on January 6, 2021. In a world increasingly urban, technological, diverse, educated, and globally connected, large swaths of America feel left behind, vulnerable, disrespected, and shamed. As Greg said, "Vulnerability is frustrating and shameful in our society. When we are feeling very vulnerable, the way we often defend against it is through violence." He concluded, regarding the insurrection: "I don't have any evidence, but I bet if I gave the participants the mattering index, most of them would end up very low on it." If modern America is willing to leave behind a large portion of its citizens increasingly unable to play by its new rules, rules shaped by globalism and technology, let's not be surprised when they are willing to break those rules.

Meeting Greg and understanding his work gave me a new lens on and language for something I had been trying to understand for quite some time: What happens when people are made to feel they do not matter? Greg helped me understand that simply getting a student into college—say, through a generous scholarship program—is not the hard work. That gets the student into the game, but if everything they experience once on campus signals to them that they do not matter to the institution and its culture, they will feel like an outsider, and their likelihood of success will decrease. It was Greg's research around that dynamic that led Brown to create a center for first-generation students. "The difficult part," he told me, "is helping them believe that they belong there."

———

Greg's work challenged Brown not only to simply spend the money to admit first-generation students—which allows them to *enter* the system—but also to make them feel like they matter, thus helping them flourish, persist, and belong. In this case, Brown created a new center focused on that challenge, with the appropriate programming so those students are recognized, invested in, and valued (Greg's three components of mattering from earlier).

If we are to fix systems, we must start with mattering—putting people back at the heart of our system design or reform. This may sound obvious, but we routinely violate that principle in education, healthcare, and our justice systems. It was a lesson I learned firsthand as a student in the Waltham, Massachusetts, public school system—then had to relearn when I became part of the higher education system.

For a long time, I thought my best teachers there were particularly gifted in making subject matter come alive in the classroom, in unlocking my learning when I struggled, in guiding my instruction. I suppose all of that is true enough. But I've come to believe that what set them apart was that they made me feel like I mattered. They got to know me as an individual, made time for me, and made me feel like my work and success were important to them. By asking more of me, holding me accountable, they were saying they believed in me and my potential. If they thought I could do the hard work, then maybe I really was more capable than I often thought.

Elizabeth Collins was a young social studies teacher who took an interest in me, giving me books in addition to the class readings because she took time to learn my interests, urged me to go to college, and then when I did, she sent me encouraging notes. Not because I was somehow outstanding—I was an uneven academic performer at best—but because every student mattered to her. Decades later, I would speak at her retirement party and thank her for the gift of her empathy and care.

I am embarrassed to admit that I lacked those gifts when I began my career as an academic. My first teaching experience was as a graduate student at Boston College teaching freshman writing. I had a star offensive lineman from the football team in my class. Let's call him Tom. Tom's brother played in the NFL, and Tom, a mountain of a kid, made the starting lineup at BC right out of high school. He was a great football player but a terrible student. His papers were painful to read, poor in thought and worse in prose, and I struggled to get through to him. Truth be told, I had some disdain for pampered athletes (my notion) and didn't try very hard, disinterested as I was in him.

His work was comically bad, including a paper on William Butler Yeats in which he called him W. B. Yeast all the way through (I couldn't resist writing "I will arise and go now" in the margins, if only for my own snarky amusement). He forgot to include any of the passages he was citing, leaving chunks of blank space throughout his paper, where I guess he intended to go back and later insert stanzas. I did not think much of Tom and largely gave up on him, writing him off as another big, dumb jock. Late in the term, the class wrote narrative essays, and Tom stunned me with his only A-level writing of the term. He wrote about how much he hated football, how his physical size and strength condemned him to play the game, how his brother's success was the only standard people applied to him, how they defined him. He explained that his father had died and that his mother attended every game, and how coming out of each huddle, he would look to find her in the stands. She was his only reason for playing and what got him through the games. It was moving and painful, and I realized that I had failed Tom as a teacher, never really getting to know him as a person or see beyond his football identity, never letting him know he mattered to me. It was worse: he didn't matter to me, and I am ashamed by my callousness. I had a long way to go to reach the standard I experienced with Mrs. Collins.

By the time I was hired as an assistant professor of English at Springfield College, I like to think that I had become a pretty good teacher. That meant knowing my field and being prepared for every class, bringing energy and passion to the classroom, working on my teaching techniques, using new teaching tools and technology, and really getting to know each of my students.

I left the faculty ranks in 1993, and the students who I still hear from, themselves the parents of college students now, are those whom I connected to outside the classroom. They remember my classes as being good (they were, I'm pretty sure). But the students we had to our house for dinner, who stayed with us when their family drama meant they had no place to go for Thanksgiving, those are the students I managed to impact more deeply.

I recently ran into a former student, now general counsel at a university, who asked me if I remembered taking him to lunch in the faculty dining room. I pretended I did. (There were countless such lunches and conversations, but I'm still a little embarrassed that I could not remember.) He described the two-hour lunch where I listened to him anguish over his career choices and the pressure his father put on him to enter the same field he had. My student said, "After that lunch, I changed my major, ended up in law school, and have a career I love. You changed my life that day." *He* changed his life that day. All I did was listen and ask questions about what *he* cared about, what *he* wanted to do someday.

Great teaching is not very much about delivering content. Yes, I want graduates to know what they need to know, but knowledge is changing and expanding at a rapid rate, and most of us learn more necessary skills in the first six months of work than in four years of classes. There are lots of engaging ways to consume content, especially as content is increasingly available and increasingly free. On the other hand, great teaching, and thus great education, is rooted in a conviction that every student matters, then acting on that conviction with time and effort.

When I ask students about their favorite faculty members, they rarely describe classes (though these faculty invariably care and are good classroom instructors) but instead describe the degree to which those faculty members know them as individuals and their interactions outside of class. While faculty members are the primary source of mattering for students, others can also play that role, including advisers, coaches, work-study supervisors, and even other students.

Mentoring programs have become a hot topic on campuses, reflecting a growing awareness of how important human relations are to overall academic success. That may sound obvious. Unfortunately, though, the reward and recognition structures of many institutions put far more weight on things like research, publishing, and disciplinary achievement than on teaching and advising.

———

For organizations that sell products or services, mattering looks like customer service. They all say they care about their customers, but how many actually communicate that in their interactions with customers?

Amazon has world-class operations and has redefined retail through its extraordinary platform, delivery, inventory, and ease of use. I never believe that I *matter* to them outside of our transactional relationship—I get what I want with unmatched ease and speed, and they get my money (and data). But when I call to get a problem resolved, the experience reinforces that I do not matter. And Apple products are marvels of good design. While they may or may not be technically better than other products, they have a cachet that a Samsung or Google phone, for example, just doesn't enjoy. I do not have any sense that Apple cares about me as a person. As long as I keep buying their products—and I do—it works well for them.

In contrast, I think about a company like Zappos, which excels at customer service. I once called because I was struggling to order shoes, and even as the customer service representative was picking up the phone, I realized my own dumb mistake in filling out the web form. I quickly explained and told her I'd let her go and just complete the order online, but she insisted that she would do it for me and was quick and efficient. At the end of the very pleasant call, she said, "I'm waiving the shipping charge." I told her she didn't have to do that, given the issue I had was of my own making and inattention, but her reply was, "Well, we probably should make that form easier if you made that mistake."

Another example: A friend and CEO had two planeloads of employees flying to the West Coast, and both flights encountered fierce headwinds requiring them to make an unscheduled fuel stop, pushing back their arrival time. On the first flight, the pilot came on the air, explained the situation, and said that everyone would get a free drink for the trouble. People scarcely looked up from their devices and books. On the second flight, the pilot said he knew people would be getting in after dinner, so there would be two dozen pizzas waiting on the jetway when they landed for fuel. The passengers broke out in applause, and my friend tells the story everywhere; it made the next day's papers. That first pilot did what he was supposed to, whereas the second pilot took the time to take better care of his passengers. I buy my shoes at Zappos still, and my friend still flies JetBlue when he can.

For organizations and systems that engage in basic human needs—education instead of phones, health instead of shoes, rehabilitation instead of flight—serving large numbers of diverse people with diverse needs and keeping individuals at the heart of the work is incredibly challenging. People often come to feel like a number, as the expression goes. As someone leading the largest university in America, I understand the tension between our desire to impact as many lives as possible—a scaling challenge that involves technology, efficiency, budgets, and more—and knowing that we have to keep individual students' lives at the heart of what we do.

In other words, we need to make sure each student feels like they matter.

SNHU has built a very large system, but it is designed to keep critical human relationships at the heart of the student experience. Most of our students are working adults who are coming back to college for a degree. They have full-time jobs, take care of kids, juggle busy lives, often with a scarcity of time and resources. About 80 percent of them tried college before. Maybe they ran out of money, maybe they were not ready to do college-level assignments, or maybe life got in the way somehow. Now, years later, they are going to give it another try.

Their greatest struggles quite often are more emotional and psychological than academic. Many failed at college once before and question if they can do the work, which has them sitting at their dining room table at 9 PM, wrestling with statistics or writing a paper for the first time in years as their family laughs at a favorite sitcom in the other room.

Being an online student can feel lonely, but every student is assigned an adviser. And while classes and faculty members change, their adviser stays with them throughout their journey, checking in, directing them to resources, solving problems with them. When that first paper comes back with a D and they throw their hands up and say, "See, I knew this was a bad idea. I'm not college material," it is the adviser who is calling, directing them to our online writing center for their next assignment, urging them to hang in there.

Along the way, advisers listen to students' stories about going through rough patches in their marriages and jobs, and their aspirations of finishing the hard task of a college education to unlock opportunity. For our students, the advising relationship affirms for them that it matters to someone that they are enrolled, that they are a student. For all the ways in which SNHU is associated with innovation and technology, our secret sauce is communicating to students this most fundamental human need: they matter.

Because advisers work directly with students, federal financial aid rules prohibit us from giving them any kind of merit bonuses, even if they are stellar. Yet they are among our most dedicated staff because of the intrinsic reward of not only making students feel like they matter, but also of knowing how much they matter to students. Many of our advisers, who often come to us as former teachers or counselors, have a sense of calling, and that is a kind of magic. It's a substantial step beyond liking one's job. It's closer to needing—aching—to do some form of work, to the point that not doing that work means being dissatisfied. It provides the fulfillment of knowing the work matters. This is an important part of the mattering equation. When systems are built to humanize the people they serve, they also humanize the people who work within the system. The served and the servers are both uplifted.

41

Of course, the opposite is also true. Systems that dehumanize the people they serve can dehumanize the people the system employs, a point most vividly demonstrated in our prison system and documented by the Marshall Project, a news organization that covers the American criminal justice system (www.themarshallproject.org). The United States imprisons a higher percentage of its population than any other industrialized nation, disproportionately jails people of color, and makes little effort to transform the lives of those inside its walls. Ken Oliver is chairman of the board of Oakland's Creating Restorative Opportunities and Programs (CROP) organization, which focuses on prisoner reentry into society. Ken served twenty-four years in prison, nine of them in solitary confinement (at first, for having a copy of a banned book, *Blood in My Eye*). He told me this about the systematic dehumanization he encountered:

Guards in the prison system in America and specifically in California mirror the behavior we see in the community with a lot of police. It's militarization. It's us against them. From the very first day they come into the [training] academy, they build that wall of "less than." "Those guys are this. Those people are that. Everything they say is a lie. Everything they say is manipulation." They attempt to strip the humanity away from people in prison to allow themselves to treat them as "less than." Those images they're taught as they go through the academy, when it's just them—they don't get to see any prisoners; it's just them—constantly reinforce this othering, eight hours a day. There's no humanity. "These people are child molesters. They're pieces of shit. They're only trying to get you to bring in a pack of cigarettes." By the time they get there, guards have their noses turned up and have preconceived notions about who you are as a human being. And it allows them to do some of the things that they do to you, which in many instances are cruel.

Ken describes an indoctrination into the system designed to make prisoners subhuman, to matter far less than those on the outside, so the use of violence or other force is acceptable. In prisons we do things to people we would never do to a human being who matters to us, such as committing them to years of solitary confinement as was done to Ken—a practice repeatedly condemned by the United Nations Committee Against Torture. As French philosopher Simone Weil explains in her essay, "The Iliad or the Poem of Force":

> How much more varied in operation, how much more stunning in effect is that other sort of force, that which does not kill, or rather does not kill just yet. It will kill for a certainty, or it will kill perhaps, or it may merely hang over the being it can kill at any instant; in all instances, it changes the human being into stone."[8]

The pervasive use of force, whether in our prisons or when a police officer kneels on the neck of a man for more than nine minutes, literally dehumanizes a person—turning them from person to thing, as Weil says. But she also points out that it comes to dehumanize those who wield that force.

Our prisons are extreme examples of what happens when systems actively dehumanize the people they ostensibly serve, as well as the people who work for and in the system. In more benign systems, say education or health care, not only can the people served by those systems feel like they do not matter, but those who work in those systems can also have their own humanity deadened. And that manifests in burnout, callousness, and a quick readiness to seize any other job that might restore energy and enthusiasm.

A physician friend recently retired and explained that he had become a doctor to work with patients but that in recent years was trying to satisfy system targets around the number of patients seen, the clinical services ordered, and billings. None of it centered on the people who needed him and, in his eyes, it diminished patient care and robbed him of the very human calling he had to the work.

———

Time and effort—always precious commodities for any busy person, whether a parent, a teacher, or a CEO—is the magic ingredient in mattering. Making time for more conversations with people, taking the time to make sure you get input from more people before making a decision, making an effort to outline all the downstream impacts of a decision, sending a personal handwritten note instead of an email when someone has had a setback or a small win at work—all of these take time and effort and have enormous payoffs.

When SNHU was smaller and I had more time, I ended most Fridays by writing two to three notes on stationary to employees, often in the lower ranks and out of the spotlight, who were doing good work. Our daughter Hannah spent one summer working with the campus landscape crew, and after work one day she told me that Elaine, the person who took care of planting flowers, kept the note I had written to her in her pocket while at work. And whenever I stay at a hotel, I leave a generous tip for the housekeeper and a note saying that my mother was a housekeeper, so I know how hard the work is and that I appreciate their effort. I have received the nicest notes in return, often with touching gratitude that I had noticed.

Everyone wants to matter, to know that their work has value to someone else. System size and scale, with the associated needs for efficiency and replicable processes, can cause them and their leaders to lose sight of that fundamental need.

As the leader of a large organization, I have seen important initiatives go off the tracks and have tried to understand why. Here's an example. We had a large group of mid-level managers working for months to think through our student experience (what a company would call the customer experience, or CX), an effort they initiated largely because they cared. They visited companies famous for their good CX, like Zappos and Disney, and they held vibrant discussions about how SNHU could improve in this area. We had brought in a talented leader to create a new line of business, and when the CX group eagerly explained that this new initiative would be the perfect place to test out their ideas, he nodded, smiled, and then dismissed the effort. The group members felt disrespected, that their work did not matter, and therefore they did not matter. Dispirited, they went back to other things. I wish this were simply the insensitivity of a new leader, but versions of that story are more common than you would think.

As I started convening groups of mid-level managers at SNHU, I learned that our meteoric growth over the last few years had resulted in more hierarchy and organizational complexity. When we were much smaller, I knew everyone's name and would see them enough that they could share their ideas. I could ask a frontline staff person how our new system or process was working. Our culture was informal enough and safe enough for that person to bring up issues, and I'd then have an opportunity to learn more and address the problems. They were helping me manage the business more effectively, and they, in turn, felt they mattered to the business. They could have an impact.

Today, my job is more external, more focused on large strategic questions, and our scope and complexity inherently mean I cannot know everyone, be everywhere, or have those informal conversations. Previously, we were small enough that my management team could enjoy that same connectedness with staff at all levels and with staff across our organizational boundaries. Now those managers have the same challenges I described for myself, and our scale means they more often stay in their own silos and have less interaction across the organization.

We have so many talented young leaders, but they tell me they often feel unheard, that leadership (I know they are thinking, *We're talking to you, boss*) makes decisions without fully understanding the implications and challenges of implementing them. One said to me, "Sometimes I wonder if the leadership team actually knows how the system works." That lack of access and consultation makes people feel that their knowledge, expertise, and input do not matter.

Similarly, when we make decisions, we are sometimes not careful to think through all the downstream implications. The impact plays out in a variety of ways. Someone gets a new assignment and does not know what to do with the current work. Perhaps they are told to stop doing one thing and do something else, regardless of how much they enjoyed the previous work or the pride they had in it. Was that work not important after all? Sometimes the required implementation demonstrates a lack of understanding of how the work actually gets done or the complexity of implementing the new thing. In all of these cases, the lack of careful thought, conversations with those impacted, and clear communication make people feel that they and their work hardly matter.

This is not to say that these types of decisions are always bad (though I'm sure we have some of those, too), but that we sometimes make them in ways that squander the considerable expertise of people at lower levels of the organization. That means we squander the opportunity to lay the groundwork for reaching an eventual decision—so decisions do not feel like they came out of nowhere—and to receive information that might improve the outcome. Early input and subsequent conversation can contribute to better implementation planning, execution, and, more importantly, better decisions in the first place. When we help people understand the *why* of a decision, how it matters within the bigger picture, and how their part of the work matters in its eventual success and impact, they are more likely to do the work well.

Against that backdrop, I am trying to understand the role of higher education and SNHU's responsibility in it—and my responsibility as the person leading the organization. How do we help our students of color imagine a better future for themselves, overcome the trauma that so many of them have experienced, inspire hope, and make them feel like they matter? We have trained our academic advisers to do trauma-informed advising but have done little in terms of culturally informed curriculum revision. While I am proud of the way we take care of students and communicate that they matter to us, I wonder if we can do more to see various student groups, particularly those from underserved communities, in their wholeness.

We have as many Native American students as the largest tribal college, but those students do not see their culture or ways of knowing reflected in their educational experience with us. On the other hand, we have dedicated admissions and advising teams for our military students, and those students routinely tell us they like SNHU because they feel their service is valued, that it matters. Can we be similarly dedicated to other groups in our student body?

Students give us high satisfaction ratings, routinely around 95 percent, but that reflects their feeling about *us*. Mattering is more about how we make them feel about themselves, with all of the positive behavioral results that a high degree of mattering yields. I am thinking here not only of their sense of well-being or self-esteem, but also of the more ineffable qualities of motivation, drive, and grit that translate into behaviors like effort, care, and academic success.

When the pandemic ended my travels in March 2020, and the chaos of that time required me to focus almost exclusively on internal matters, I included in my work frequent drop-ins with teams across the university to reassure them and see what they needed. It was, in some ways, a virtual version of my walks around the office from a previous era.

We had just created a team to work on the next generation of our digital platform, and someone not on that team casually commented about its members, saying, "They're pretty excited about the project but don't know how long before we pull the plug on it." I was confused, and when the team next met with me, I asked if that comment accurately described a concern. There were a lot of exchanged glances on the video call, and one brave soul said, "Yes, we do that a lot at SNHU" and provided examples. In each example, I knew the rationale for what had changed, why we redirected an effort, and how we reached the decision. But that didn't really matter. What did matter was that this group of some of our very best people did not understand those decisions and felt that they knew things that could have usefully informed leadership's thinking but had never been asked. As a result, they were going into this important new work with a kind of tepid commitment and a deeper unease about leadership. A subtext to their comments was wondering if their work mattered, and, by extension, if they mattered enough. Perhaps I was reading too much into that last bit, but as I listened to this group, I realized that each member felt a bit adrift in our organization. It was not a good feeling.

If we learn best from our failings, then this is a rich opportunity for me. First, the pandemic was a gift in that it plugged me back into the organization I lead. One faculty member said, "We used to run into you all the time on campus and check in, ask questions, and just connect. We miss that." I thus began weekly video chats with various faculty groups, which have been invaluable as we reimagine our campus programs.

The campus is a small part of our overall organization, serving some three thousand students, less than 2 percent of our total student population. Like most residential campuses, it runs an operating deficit and needs some rethinking about its underlying business model. My conversations with faculty have revealed all that one might expect in these circumstances: fear of change, concerns for job security, and a desire to hold on to what they most love about their campus life. The unspoken piece is the need for reassurance that the brick-and-mortar campus still matters, even if the online division is the university's economic engine. The faculty want reassurance that their opinions matter and will be considered in the reengineering of the campus. By recalling a time when we ran into each other and chatted, they were recalling a time when they felt they mattered more.

I was reminded of a 1999 *New York Times Magazine* piece about John Casteen, the legendary president of the University of Virginia who raised what was then a record amount of money for a public university. And that meant he was rarely on campus, earning him criticism. As a colleague said, "It doesn't matter that you raised $10 million yesterday; if a faculty member has to jump through hoops to get a printer cartridge, it's going to feel like you aren't paying attention."

The conversations I am having with faculty and staff might be good for them in terms of feeling valued, but they are also exceedingly good for me in terms of my learning and informing my discussions at the leadership team level. I need these conversations more than the faculty and staff do.

As we think about improving and rehumanizing systems, getting it right means that the people we serve believe that they matter—that we know them, invest in them, and value them. When we do it well, our own people will also be uplifted. Indeed, they need to feel like they matter if they are going to do the same for the people they serve, or as we often say at SNHU, "If we treat our people well, they will treat our students well."

We are the only university in America to be listed on the *Chronicle of Higher Education*'s Great Colleges to Work For list every year since its inception. Our students and recent graduates routinely give us 95 percent satisfaction ratings. Those two ratings are deeply connected. My point is that mattering is an essential human need, but it is also at the heart of good system design.

When Dr. Lorris Betz was the CEO of University of Utah Health, his wife had a sudden and acutely painful case of kidney stones. He described the situation to me:

> The receptionist—the triage person at the emergency room—said, "OK, go over there, sit down, and we'll call you when we're ready." My wife told the receptionist, "I'm going to vomit." She was sitting there and grabbed a pencil tray and gave it to my wife to vomit into. Then they still made us sit for about an hour or so before we got back to see somebody when it was really pretty clear what the problem was. She got a CT scan, which showed a kidney stone. The resident could see it there right away. But it took another hour before the radiologist read it. They were then able to ask a urologist to take a look at her. The urologist comes in and didn't even introduce herself to us. She just came in and said, "Yep, you have a kidney stone. I think we're going to do this, this, this, this." They needed one of

those kidney stone smasher devices called a lipotripser. It took three hours for them to get access to it. Eventually, she had it done. It just took a long, long time for us to get in a position to leave. It all seemed so useless. I was there by her side watching this the whole time.

Remember, this is the spouse of the system CEO. Soon thereafter, while leaving for vacation, his wife had a recurrence of sharp pain, and he pulled the car over. He called the hospital and left voice mails, tried the urology clinic where patients were treated, and had the hospital operator page the physician who had seen her. He recalled, "So here we were in Ogden, Utah, on the side of the road, and in pain, and I couldn't get anybody to talk to us about it."

Lorris, as the leader of the system, did not blame others. In his comments to me, he blamed himself for letting the system evolve into this state of affairs. When he returned to work, he threw himself into the data—patient surveys—for a look under the hood.

I started going to meetings all over the place, talking about how terrible this was. I did videos that could be shown at meetings all across the institution. I got all our department chairs energized around this as well. The people in the hospital—the nurses, the technicians, even the room keepers who clean the rooms afterward—really got into this quickly.

Lorris organized task forces, encouraged experiments and innovations, and worked on the culture—work we will return to in a later chapter. While that was critical to reforming the system, he said that in the end what mattered most was making patients feel like they really mattered to Utah Health:

What really resonated with the hospital staff was that we were doing a poor job of meeting our patients' needs. The phrase that

51

we used a lot was *medical care can only be truly great if the patient thinks it is.* So there was a focus on what the patient wants. We started asking questions: What are you worried about? What do you care most about? What's important to you? It's the questions they hadn't been asked before, and patients responded to that very, very positively.

While they said it in various ways, Lorris said the basic response of patients was, "I want to be treated with respect."

Respect, care, and a sense that they matter. That's what we try to give our students at SNHU. As higher education increasingly moves from the analog to the digital, we are investing enormous amounts of money into our technology, our platforms, our processes, and trying to take the manual and the human out of all the places where an algorithm will improve our students' experiences.

The most critical question we face in that effort, the one we can't get wrong, is where human relations must remain in the student experience. We know, for example, that many students would prefer a seamless consumer-grade experience when navigating routine administrative processes; they'd rather have something like Amazon's one-click shopping than to be on a phone with one of our staff. However, we have to give students human interaction and use technology to free up our staff to do more of those impactful interactions and to do them better.

Increasingly, that requires us to harness data analytics and personalization to build individual student profiles at scale. Then we can use technology to proactively signal when a student needs us and to better understand the nature of that need. We are building the platform for that work, using industry-leading customer relationship management technology. Visitors are often fascinated with that aspect of our student advising, but I always remind them that the technology amplifies and improves the impact of the human interactions it supports. We increasingly expect the sort of seamless transactional experience of an Amazon, but we are moved when we get actual care that communicates we matter. That's the secret sauce of our work.

———

If we are to rehumanize organizations and systems, we must begin with mattering—for those whom we serve and those whom we employ. Using Greg Elliott's three fundamental questions, we might ask ourselves:

- How do our people (our students, patients, inmates, and staff) know that we know they exist? Do we see them? Recognize them? Listen to them?
- How are we investing in them? Do they feel like we are wringing out of them every possible dollar? Are we giving them our time? Are we in genuine conversation with them?
- Do they feel valued? How do they see their needs, desires, and ideas reflected in the system and organizations we lead?

We have watched a steady and profound erosion of trust in systems—from schools to government institutions to criminal justice to the industry that I know and love, higher education. These entities are often seen as self-serving, out of touch with the people they serve, and as part of the problem in America rather than part of the solution.

The question I asked at the start of this exploration was, Can higher education learn to love its students again? Some responded to me with "did it ever?" I think it did. I think it can again. But like other systems that have lost their way, it will have to begin with the most fundamental need we all have—the need to matter. But that's not enough, and the chapters to come will build on this idea.

53

No system of care can succeed if it does not satisfy this core desire to matter in a world that can often feel dehumanized, callous, and uncaring. The revolutionary power of early Christianity, the Enlightenment, and the American experiment was that we as individuals matter, that everyone matters. Capitalism, especially as practiced in post-Reagan-era America, with its power-of-markets fetishism, has substituted shareholder value, efficient use of capital, and regulatory freedom for mattering. That may be acceptable in commercial systems of goods and services, but it is ill-suited for the more vital and human-centered work of caring for our vulnerable, educating our citizens, and helping all people realize their potential in ways that uplift them and make them matter more.

DREAMING BIGGER DREAMS

P aul could go to college someday."

That sentence changed everything for me. Mark Schlafman, my sixth-grade teacher, said it to my mother in a parent-teacher conference, and it inspired a dream for her—and for me—that had never really occurred to us before. No one in our family had gone to college. No one in our working-class neighborhood, either. On the South Side of Waltham, most men worked in construction or performed other physical labor, most women worked at home, and a good job was one sheltered from the elements. A great job was working for the city or state, with the stability and eventual pension it carried. College was for other people's kids.

I didn't know those kids, but I knew where they lived. My mother cleaned their houses.

Because of my Acadian heritage, my first language was French—well, as much language as a three-year-old has—and when my mother would clean the houses of wealthy people in the tony Boston suburbs of Weston and Wayland, she would bring me along and sit me down in beautiful wood-paneled libraries and take children's books down from the shelves to keep me distracted while she vacuumed and dusted and washed sinks and toilets. These are some of my earliest and happiest childhood memories, the smell of leather bindings and polished wood, being nestled in soft cushions on a window seat (I had never seen a window seat!) looking out on a woodsy backyard with a book in hand and my mother's soft singing wafting in from an adjacent room as she cleaned. I graduated from simple picture books to children's books and eventually to the L. Frank Baum *Wizard of Oz* series long before I was capable of really understanding them.

Almost all those memories go back to the home of Mr. and Mrs. Thompson, the couple for whom my mother worked the longest and whose library had the Baum books I still fondly remember. They were Protestant. In my Catholic family, that was a designation associated with wealth, power, and the English (who my father still disliked from his World War II days, when French Canadian units were often led by English-speaking officers and used as cannon fodder). The Thompsons had a beautiful house that today would seem modest but felt like a mansion to me at the time. My own family today teases me about my love for wall-to-wall carpeting, but I remember the Thompsons had it in their wondrous home. It was warm and soft underfoot, and I still somehow associate it with luxury no matter how currently passé it is.

My mother became kind of a friend to Mrs. Thompson. I say "kind of" because there was affection and a sharing of confidences, but an employer-employee relationship is not the unconditional intimacy of equals. Yet Mrs. Thompson took a kindly interest in me, often suggesting books and praising the artwork I'd leave for her. It was the first hint of feeling believed in by someone who wasn't one of my parents. She put more books in front of me, books that often pushed me beyond my language and comprehension. They opened up new worlds, allowed me to live the lives of characters foreign to me and my family, and let me visit places so different from the one we inhabited.

The Thompsons used an antique cobbler's bench as a coffee table in their study and the latest issues of *National Geographic* and *Life* magazines were always on it. My lifelong passion for travel, passed down to my daughters, has its roots in those magazines and the windows into exotic worlds they provided. I know people who in tough childhoods found refuge in books, but I had a loving family and happy childhood. We were the working poor (though I didn't know it then), but jobs were plentiful, my parents worked incredibly hard and saved, and my modest needs were all filled. Books for me were flights of imagination, less about escape than adventure.

Mrs. Thompson not only opened up my world, but in giving me a bit of her time, in praising me, in telling me I was smart, she made me feel capable. All of that mattered more because of who she was, where she stood in my world. She represented class, prestige, and power, which we could only glimpse from the edges. If she said these things to me, they just might be true, and that was the beginning of believing in myself.

Likewise, Mr. Schlafman enjoyed hero status in my world. He knew most of the Boston Celtics during the glory years in the 1960s (and later went on to become an NBA referee), a time when they were dominating the league and were local sports legends. He gave us Celtics gear and the Christmas cards they sent him so we could have the players' autographs (John Havlicek was mine). He took an interest in me and pushed me to do tougher work, making sure I was in the top tier for seventh grade the next year, at a time when grouping students by perceived aptitude was common and apparent to all. Grade 7-1 (code for Grade 7, Level 1) was for the smart kids who might go to college someday, and he made sure I was among them. I don't know what he saw in me then, but I suspect it was my unabashed love for books and my curiosity, the source of all love of learning. When Mr. Schlafman said to my mother, "Paul could go to college someday," he invited her to imagine a different life for me. Mr. Schlafman's and Mrs. Thompson's belief in my potential germinated something in me.

————

As much as financial poverty stands in the way of young people going to college, poverty of aspiration is more insidious. Financial poverty is mechanical, transactional, and can be addressed if we as a society muster the will. We can create financial aid systems far better than the one we have and make sure that lack of funds do not keep poor kids from attending college. That's poverty of the wallet. Poverty of aspiration diminishes the heart and the mind. The lack of belief in oneself, and the inability to dream bigger dreams, chokes a child's potential before it is even visible.

Aspiration is something nurtured and undergirded by imagination, confidence, resiliency, and mattering. While every child is born with the potential for all four, it is not certain they will meet the people or circumstances that will enable them to aspire greatly. Larry Bacow, the president of Harvard University, and I were driving together and sharing the stories of our parents and our journeys. Larry's parents were also immigrants, his mother the only member of her family to escape Auschwitz, while his father and his family came to the US to escape pogroms in Eastern Europe. He commented that we had both experienced the American Dream. That dream was more available to us than it was to many others even then because we were White and male and despite our humble beginnings, we attended public schools when America still believed in public education and funded it accordingly. We had loving parents and influential teachers who believed in and challenged us. We could aspire.

We were lucky. Far too many children in America grow up in dream-crushing circumstances, where structural racism and poverty have destroyed communities and wreaked havoc on families. A large body of research shows that young people come to accept stereotypes about whatever group to which they belong.[1] For young Black children, acceptance of racial stereotypes about them has been shown to lower academic achievement. As one meta study outlines, "the most serious outcomes of long-term disidentification include dropping out of school and displaying disruptive behavior in the classroom . . . Thus, stereotype threat can potentially influence both short-term disengagement and long-term disidentification with academics."[2]

The insidious danger here is not simply being told that you will not amount to much, but believing the stereotype yourself, internalizing it, then confirming it with poor performance, disengagement, and lowered expectations for what is possible. Black and Latinx youth are far more likely to be neither in school nor in the workforce than their White peers and report feelings of hopelessness and depression at higher rates.[3]

That crisis of hopelessness has come to impact much of America, and not just children from stigmatized groups. Increasing hopelessness is reflected in everything from suicide rates, decreasing longevity, prescriptions for anxiety medication and antidepressants, substance abuse, and mental illness. In May 2020, the Centers for Disease Control and Prevention recorded the highest number of deaths from overdose in any twelve-month period, with eighteen jurisdictions reporting increases greater than 50 percent. Even more alarming, ten western states reported increases in synthetic opioid-involved deaths of 98 percent.[4] The CDC has also reported that the rate of suicide for those ages ten to twenty-four increased nearly 60 percent between 2007 and 2018. Suicide became the second leading cause of death among people ages ten to thirty-four in 2018.[5]

In a globally connected, technology-driven knowledge economy, the lack of a meaningful postsecondary degree increasingly means being condemned to poorly paid low-skill work. Increasingly rare are the well-paying middle-skill jobs that allowed a generation of post–World War II Americans to build middle-class lives through blue-collar jobs. Unions have long been on the decline, manufacturing was sent abroad, and the US economy is fueled by technology, finances, and services.

As people and jobs have moved to the coasts and urban areas, rural America and the industrial centers of the Midwest have been devastated. With lives lived on the edge, the once proud protagonists of the American narrative—farmers, ranchers, and factory workers—find themselves marginalized in hollowed-out communities, suffering a kind of shame that drives many of them to nativist populism, blaming the "other," and embracing a nostalgic view of the past because of their inability to see a future for themselves. Anyone born in the last twenty years has only known perpetual war, two recessions, a pandemic, dysfunctional and divisive politics, and the existential threat of climate change. Is it any wonder that we have record levels of hopelessness, substance abuse, and suicide?

So much of the discussion in postsecondary education is about things we can readily fix—aligning education to labor force needs, affordability, and assessment, for example—but the fundamental issue we face is a country of people giving up. They are losing their ability to imagine a better future, their belief in themselves has eroded, and they feel like they do not matter. There is ample evidence that they are too often right on this last point, especially in communities of color and the working poor. But historically high levels of anxiety and depression now afflict all demographic groups, exacerbated by the pandemic. My worst days as a university president were the ones in which I had to call the mothers of students who had taken their own lives.

The power of aspiration and hope might be best appreciated in those places where it is in shortest supply. SNHU has an ambitious program to bring full-degree programs to displaced people through its Global Education Movement program, working with refugees in Rwanda, Kenya, South Africa, Malawi, and Lebanon. People are often shocked to learn that the average stay of a refugee now approaches twenty years and that whole generations may be born and die in a camp. Of the world's eighty-four million refugees, 75 percent are dispersed in urban areas, living in squalor without access to basic services, and often victimized.[6]

In 2019, I traveled to the Kakuma Refugee Camp run by the United Nations High Commission on Refugees, which houses over two hundred thousand refugees, many of whom have only ever known life in the camp. While there, I met Ignazio Matteini, the charismatic Italian UNHCR official who was heading the camp then. We were introduced to two students who were struggling emotionally and psychologically, and our team was fearful for them. The US under the Trump administration had virtually halted any refugee repatriation, and people were losing hope with that news. The suicide rate at Kakuma was increasing at an alarming rate. We decided to give these two young men full scholarships to come study on our US campus. Ignazio and his team joined us when we gave them the news. He recalled:

I think it was one of the most moving moments when we announced that they got the scholarships. The reaction of the two was completely different. One started talking and wouldn't stop because he had to find a way to stop the emotions and not cry. The other one just broke down in silent tears. He couldn't say anything. It was not even sobbing—the tears were just coming out. The different emotions of the two were in reality the same emotion.

It was a feeling of being overwhelmed with hope and a sense of the future. I'm not a psychologist, but it was really a big impact moment for us. It brought hope to them and to the other refugees but also to the people who had been working with them for years. Not everywhere do they have these opportunities to see something like that. We should have gotten cameras and shared that with all the people of the world because that was a moment of emotional breakthrough for all of us.

I was deeply affected by that moment but also gutted that we were only helping two. I was overwhelmed by the magnitude of the problem and the depth of human suffering and struggle we had witnessed. Ignazio took me aside and said, "You have to understand you are changing the lives of these two young men, but you are also giving hope to everyone else. Giving hope—that is the most valuable currency you can make available."

Former US Secretary of Education Arne Duncan is in the business of giving hope to young men trapped in a deadly cycle of violence in south and west Chicago. He is the founder of Chicago CRED (short for Creating Real Economic Destiny), a nonprofit that combines street outreach, workforce development, and advocacy to fight against gun violence. It begins its transformative work with one-on-one counseling. As the CRED website, www.chicagocred.org, says, "By understanding how trauma affects the body and mind, and learning how to respond to intense emotions with nonaggressive actions, men are better equipped to cope with their past and become productive members of society."

Arne spends his days working with people who live in crime-ridden neighborhoods that have not gotten better over the last decades and have arguably gotten worse. He said that on the day before we spoke, he was talking to a man who "wasn't even sure if he had ten or twelve bullet holes. He said he doesn't remember. He has been shot in five different incidents." For that young man, Arne said, "it is not an irrational thing to think that you're not going to have a long life."

I asked Arne if he is helping the young men at Chicago CRED rewrite their stories. He said,

I wouldn't say rewriting. It's just that there are more chapters. We have guys write their autobiographies, and they are real and raw and pretty moving. We do a public reading so we don't whitewash anything or hide from something . . . Maybe the most important thing we do is try to help people heal and deal with trauma and not paint over it or cover it up. It's less of a rewrite. It's just that there are many chapters to go, many innings still to play.

Part of what Chicago CRED does is help young men envision a better world than the only one they have known and give them the tools to realize it. When we first explored offering college degree pathways to those men, we wondered how much interest there might be. Arne reached out to me, surprised at the response, and said both the men and the staff wanted that option.

Dennis Littky is founder of the groundbreaking Metropolitan School (the Met, as it's known), a high school that was created to take the kids no one else wanted, and College Unbound, a new institution based on the principles he used at the Met that serves a similar, if older demographic. Dennis said to me,

If I get out of prison, I walk the streets as a felon. If I get out of prison and enroll in College Unbound, I walk the streets as a college student. What people expect of me, and what I expect of myself, differs greatly with those two identities. As a felon, I'm imprisoned by my past. As a college student, I am focused on my future.

Throughout my career as an educator and to this day, I ponder what it is that instills in some students a curiosity and desire for learning while others remain uninterested. More than being uninterested, I wonder why they seem to believe in themselves less than I believe in them. Why do they not aspire to learn, to stretch themselves, to understand worlds not their own, to desire a better and more enriched life than the one they seem to accept? Student apathy, lack of curiosity and drive, and willingness to do only enough confounds me. I often wonder if they lacked a Mr. Schlafman or a Mrs. Thompson, if they were not invited to imagine a better world to which they could aspire. Did they not have the teachers I had, the ones who communicated "there is a big and wondrous world out there, and you can be part of it?"

When I was a doctoral student at the University of Massachusetts in Amherst, I studied composition and rhetoric, taught writing courses, and researched the impact of technology on literacy behaviors. One study of students in Massachusetts revealed that when given more time to revise their writing, most students did not improve their drafts and many actually made them worse. The researchers concluded that time for revision was only useful if one could imagine a better version of the essay. In a similar way, how can young people aspire to a world they simply do not know?

———

Dr. Matt Biel is the chief of Child and Adolescent Psychiatry and Pediatrics at Georgetown University Medical Center. We were discussing this puzzle of resiliency, and he suggested that at the core, it requires three things:

1. That a person has some passion—for almost anything, but something that lights them up.

2. That they have one good year where things are "normal," even if things later go back to being bad. That year anchors a dream of a situation better than the one they find themselves in.

3. That they have someone who believes in them.

That last item particularly resonates with me. If asked to list the most influential people in our lives, most happy adults would list one or more teachers. Almost always, they describe a teacher who took an interest in them, who got to know them as a young person, and who challenged and supported them to realize a better version of themselves. It isn't always a teacher; those lists can also include coaches, club advisers, work-study supervisors, and staff with whom students connected.

One of the central challenges with which I wrestle at SNHU is how to hold on to that essential truth at scale. Skeptics often ask me, "How can SNHU really support individual students at such numbers?" It's hard and a work in progress for us.

A bit of background: The majority of our online learners are nontraditional-age learners: our typical student is twenty-eight years old, holds down a full-time job, and is a parent. We have over thirty thousand students of color and thousands of Native American students. Eighty percent of our students have tried college before and come to us with credits, often from more than one place. They never completed college—perhaps they ran out of money, life got in the way, an opportunity presented itself, or they just weren't ready—and they usually have some student debt. Almost one in five served in the military. We are an open-admissions university, caring more about getting students across the finish line than worrying about where they start the race. Most of our students are considering college because they are stuck. They need an opportunity, a better job to take care of their families and themselves. So they call us.

We pay attention to the same components of learning that any other good university does, like learning design, pedagogy, the learning platform and supports, and hiring and training effective instructors. We start with an assumption that we need to help students learn, but all (or almost all) are capable. As Dr. Matt Steinfeld, an assistant professor of psychiatry at the Yale School of Medicine, argues, students are already designed for learning. He asks, "How is it possible that someone is not learning given that we are designed to learn?" He answers, "Trauma, structural racism, poverty, working around the clock—all these structural forces and the way we internalize them and reproduce them in ourselves get in the way of the natural process of learning."

We have learned that unlocking that inherent predilection to learn requires relationships, conversation, and understanding. It means putting the student at the heart of the work—not just in terms of academics, but as whole human beings with all the baggage they carry. At SNHU, it has taken us years to build a human-focused system that assumes all can learn but that most need encouragement, personal support and attention, and often a reminder of the bigger goal. We are still not good enough at it for some of our most in-need learners, often those who have the lowest incomes and little social capital. For example, our graduation rate for low-income Black students still lags behind our overall graduation. Students who start with zero credits previously earned and who are brand-new to college still struggle mightily. For all the data we collect—and we collect more than most places—we are not yet as good as we need to be for too many of our students.

It really isn't so much the practical and transactional supports that students need—though those are important—but belief in possibility. It is hard to overstate the importance of that first conversation with an SNHU admissions counselor. Prospective students have lots of practical and important questions: What will it cost? How can I pay for it? How many of my prior credits will count? What's the right program for me? How do I know this is a good school? Can online education work for me? Will employers respect my degree? What's this process like?

The counselors' first task is to provide clear information and guidance, and to answer their questions. There is, however, a bigger and often unstated set of questions at play. They revolve around confidence, resolve, capacity, and doubt. Often, students' stories include the kind of trauma that Steinfeld references: life journeys that include poverty, failure, struggle, and victimization at the hands of others and sometimes at the hands of systems. So much of that first conversation is about helping students see themselves as college students, even if they failed at earlier attempts or don't look like the kids in college brochures or have been told all their lives they don't have what it takes. We have to help them sort out the practical questions, but we also have to give them hope.

When students enroll, they are assigned an academic adviser who, with the aid of a powerful technology platform that helps track student progress and flags any of the warning signs of struggle, is at the students' side throughout their journey at SNHU. While they, too, have practical tasks associated with their students' progress—getting them registered in the right courses, confirming they have the right prerequisites, pointing them to additional academic resources if needed—so much of their work is about the emotional and psychological baggage that students carry. When a new student gets a poor grade on the first writing assignment they've completed in ten years, it's easy for them to throw up their hands and say, "See, I knew I wasn't college material. What was I thinking, coming back to school?" At that moment, the adviser plays a critical role, reminding them that those skills are, of course, rusty, suggesting they use our online writing center to review drafts before they submit their next paper, and encouraging them not to give up. Advisers check in with students, encouraging and sometimes cajoling. They listen to students worried about struggles at work, a sick child, an annoying spouse (or worse). During the pandemic, students who were also frontline health-care workers would often share heartbreaking stories of dying patients with their academic advisers so they could be unburdened with their families, a heavy load for our advisers to carry. Advisers are our heroes.

It would be easy to confuse what our advisers do with good customer service, but it is much more substantial and complex, situated in deep relationships. Steinfeld draws an analogy to counseling:

> It's really important for the young clinicians we train to understand that part of our task is—to lean on Carl Sagan—to light the candle in the darkness, to evoke the sacred from the mundane. When someone comes in and their life is a disaster, what can we draw on in the consulting room together to spark some hope, some future orientation?

He describes our advisers as "holding space" for someone to re-catalyze the learning process:

> We're meant to learn. We're meant to grow. Traumas, a lack of opportunity, disrupt that natural process. So we don't have to create a new process. We have to restart something that's indigenous in all of us given the right conditions ... Seeds when put in the earth and given some sunlight and water will grow. Structural inequities in our society make growth very hard. Part of what [advisers] do is keep a felt pulse on who your learners are as people.

That often starts with overcoming the internalized baggage that they carry with them. Sara Goldrick-Rab, the highly regarded founder of the Hope Center for College Community and Justice in Philadelphia and a professor of sociology and medicine at Temple University, often works with students suffering food and housing insecurity and who are just hanging on to their college dream. She told me,

> A lot of the work I do with students is when they're very close to the bottom, and there's a lot of talk of just throwing it all away—and I mean throw away college or throw away life, both sometimes. The only ones who make it through are the ones who find the "why." I have a strategy I use over and over with almost every student. I asked them about the ways they feel beaten down and who has beaten them down. And then I say, "Why do you think this keeps happening?" They'll often say, "Well, I make bad decisions." They live in America, so of course they internalize it. It's what we do.

Sara says her students "lose their aspirations and their bigger dreams very early." When they finally understand that their struggles are built into systems that are ostensibly there to serve them, she says they "start to fight the system and find the resolve to beat the system" and once again aspire to a better life.

When that turnaround begins, when we have held the space for and with students, have processed the traumas, and have "seen" them fully as people, we have to also give them role models. Seeing others realize similar dreams makes those dreams real. Sara also echoes the point Ignazio made about our two lucky students in the Kakuma Refugee Camp being models for others, when she says, "There really is something important in having role models. You have to have examples of success, and how would you know that you could ever do these things if you've never seen anybody like you do them?"

The power of role models is a critical component of the innovative work done by Groups Recover Together, a health-care company specializing in opioid addiction treatment with success rates two to three times higher than the rest of the industry. CEO Colleen Nicewicz talks about the importance of group therapy for members (the term they use for clients) just starting treatment, as they see others further along and having success:

> When you have a good group with members who have been there for different lengths of time, the counselors can almost sit back and let the rest of the members talk and provide the guidance. As a new member, I can see myself in somebody who's a year sober, and I'm only a month in. "I want to be like that. If I keep at it, I'll be like them. That's what it's going to be like, and this is what I have to do to get there." To be able to see your treatment pathways in somebody who you really relate to, who lives in your community, who you see at the grocery store? It is incredibly powerful.

There is power in seeing one's dreams realized in others. In our work with students, we need to remind the struggling learner of the bigger aspiration, of why they are doing this hard work, of what happens when they are successful. At SNHU, our television commercials almost always feature shots of joyous graduates and commencement ceremonies. It's an invitation for prospective students to see themselves in those robes, to see themselves as college graduates. In the commercials' thirty- and sixty-second moments, they do what Mr. Schlafman did for my mother and me by allowing people to see themselves as college graduates someday.

———

There is some irony that many outside SNHU describe us as one of the most innovative universities in higher education—often citing our use of data or technology or new delivery models—when our success depends so much on meeting deeply human needs such as mattering, hope, and resiliency. Yes, to do that at scale requires us to harness technology and data, but we do that to amplify human interactions and make them more impactful, not to replace them with lower cost technological solutions. Because the human work is grounded in the messiness of human nature, with all of its wonder and frustration, it is actually the hardest part of the educational endeavor and also the most magical.

The most elite universities take the top 1 percent of high school graduates, students wired for academic success and often from privileged backgrounds. They compete with each other to enroll the best of the best within that 1 percent. We are open admissions, taking nearly all who want to try. For some, we are almost the only viable option. We serve refugees in some of the most godforsaken places on the globe. We serve DACA students in the Rio Grande Valley and homeless kids in LA County. We serve men and women who were deployed on our behalf to Iraq and Afghanistan. When they walk across the stage to get their degrees, I see in their faces so much emotion. I see the physical manifestation of human transformation, hope realized. That takes genuine human relationships, knowing our students, and time.

Whether working in substance abuse, counseling as Matt Steinfeld and Colleen do, helping marginalized college students as Sara does, or trying to save young men from gun violence as Arne does, the work is centered on human relations. There is no efficiency play, no substitute for time, no algorithm for holding someone else's past or their dreams for their future. As Sara commented, "What you can't do with students is just quickly extract everything you need from them. There are those who think teaching is just pouring knowledge into empty vessels, but it is incredibly relational, and it requires spending time with students."

When those students carry trauma, the time needed to serve them well grows exponentially. "It's a much heavier experience," Sara explains, "and I can't just shrug off a student. It takes a lot more time to do what

I do with those students." The struggle for time is a common theme across most systems. For example, Colleen's company had to persuade health insurance companies to cover more time in group sessions.

Therein lies the central challenge to all systems that seek to serve people at scale, whether it's health care, the K–12 system, the judicial system, or a place like SNHU: the larger the organization or system, the more its operation requires standardization, efficiency, replicable processes, and levels of oversight. Bureaucracy sets in. There's a lot to manage, so a lot of managers get hired and layers accrue. Communication becomes more difficult.

When SNHU was small, I could walk the halls, know everyone's name. An entry-level person could pull me aside to tell me about a struggling student and ask for support to intervene in some way or another. At 2,500 students, our organization could really know our students. At one hundred eighty thousand students and with over thirteen thousand employees, the organization necessarily relies on data, on cohort modeling, on categories (and thus labels), and we build our services and support for scale. Through sheer numbers and layers of people and specialized functions, more and more of a system's people are removed from the actual people the system serves.

The danger is that the ability to know people as individuals, to give them time, to provide what they need in the ways they need it (not the ways the system prefers to deliver) degrades and gives way to the needs of the system to be efficient and scalable. As Gary Hamel and Michele Zanini point out in the wonderful book *Humanocracy*, "bureaucracies are complex, integrated systems. Every process is connected to every other process. This lack of modularity makes it difficult to change one thing without changing everything."[7] Those processes, often piling one upon another, start to require people within the system to attend to them rather than to the people the system actually serves. A recent SNHU internal report illustrates the impact:

> Staff feedback highlights that multiple levels of approval are required for tasks that are either routine or close to routine. With each subsequent level of approval comes a delay that can impact students and staff. For example, the process to seek approval can be inefficient with lots of waiting, steps requiring stakeholder approval can make completing tasks difficult, and processes across Global Campus—from scholarship requests to academic petitions—are delayed by multiple steps with multiple sign-offs.

As Hamel and Zanini observe, "staff groups justify their existence by issuing rules and mandates, which seldom have a sunset clause. As a result, the clog of red tape grows ever bigger."[8] They quote famous German sociologist Max Weber: "Bureaucracy develops more perfectly the more it is 'dehumanized,' the more it succeeds in eliminating all purely personal, irrational, and emotional elements which escape calculation."[9]

Hamel and Zanini are focused on the dehumanization of employees. A 2019 Gallup poll showed that globally only 15 percent of workers feel engaged by their work and, while better, that number is still only 30 percent in the US.[10] And that was before the pandemic, which has seen millions of people refusing to return to dehumanizing jobs in what some have called the Great Resignation.[11]

It would be easy to assign that refusal to do dehumanizing work to the lowest levels of an organization—hourly workers in retail or food service, for example—but in his last book before he died in 2020, *Bullshit Jobs*, noted anarchist anthropologist David Graeber points out that some 40 percent of white-collar workers believe their jobs are meaningless and would not be missed if they went away tomorrow.[12]

My worry for SNHU is that with our large size, we are asking our frontline people to do too much bureaucratic work instead of life-changing work (for them and their students), and if we dehumanize their jobs, requiring them to spend more of their time satisfying the system and its needs, they will in turn have less time for the humanizing work they do with students. I know one physician after another who has come to feel that way about the systems in which they work and the ways in which they can no longer serve patients (especially not having enough time to spend with them).

The challenge my team and I are taking on is how do we, at scale, make sure students feel like they matter? How do we help them dream bigger dreams for themselves, which takes time to really know them? How do we give them what they need to be successful, which means giving our people who work with students the time and freedom required to give students what they need while also making our system work?

Compared to other providers serving the same student populations, we do it better than most. But that is a low bar, and too many students do not complete their education. So we continue to work on improving, and I am increasingly convinced that the system does not hold the answers.

Outside observers sometimes think that the lesson we have taken from our success in online education is that virtual education works well (it does!) and that we have somehow mastered the application of technology and data (sort of true). We certainly apply technology to the work of reimagining our delivery models and investing in machine learning, data analytics, virtual reality, and more. But we also have learned a basic lesson that every true educator knows and too many technophiles forget: people and human relationships, not technology, are key to transformable educational experiences. As our organization grows and the system takes on a life of its own, we are in a constant battle to keep that lesson front and center for our students and employees.

I wish that challenge was only true for scaled organizations like ours, but the postsecondary education system has evolved to serve itself more than students. Much of higher education has long lost its focus on students to its own self-interest, including the admissions process that high school students have to endure, the one-size-fits-all idea of the major and rigid curricular structures, the cost of attendance, the outdated pedagogies, and a "we know what's best for you" arrogance. It is left to heroic individuals to do the right thing for students, and too many students move through the system never discovering or being discovered by the kind of gifted faculty that believed in me, got to know me, and dared me to dream bigger dreams for myself.

We have to be better. That said, our efforts to rethink education have to start and rest with these core human questions of hope and aspiring to a better world. I was given the gift of having those qualities nurtured in me, as did so many of my peers. It is the gift we must give our students because those qualities are the foundation of all learning and all systems meant to lift people up.

———

Asad Hardwick came to SNHU from the Roxbury neighborhood of Boston. His father had long been out of his life. His mother struggled with substance abuse and had been evicted as a result. His brother had been shot and was in a wheelchair. Asad was essentially homeless, finally taken in by Pops, the chef and owner of a small takeout restaurant where Asad worked part-time. Asad enrolled in the METCO program, which bused him two hours each way to high school in Foxborough, a White and relatively affluent suburb. Asad later told me that while his

Roxbury friends were dealing drugs, joining gangs, and being jailed or shot, Foxborough allowed him to see a different world, a set of possibilities he had not imagined before.

A letter from Asad showed up in my mail pile one day after he had applied to SNHU. He explained his situation, said he had fallen in love with the university and had connected with our head of diversity programs, Louisa Martin. Our financial aid offer had arrived, he said, and he had no way to fill the gap between our cost and what his aid package offered. Such letters are not uncommon, but what was different is that Asad asked if he could work more and pay off his tuition over a longer period of time. He did not simply ask for more grant money, as so many students in that situation do. I was struck by his desire to work and his positivity. I called Admissions and asked about him. They said they were really taken with him and had maxed out the financial aid formulas in every way they could. I then called Louisa and asked her about Asad. She raved about him.

I called him while he was in the middle of making a delivery for Pops, so he pulled over. I explained who I was and shared what our team had said about him, and that I would give him a Presidential Scholarship for the balance of his funding, no additional work needed. He later told me that his girlfriend was in the van with him and kept asking him, "What is it?" as he sat in stunned silence, trying not to cry. Foxborough had allowed him to see a world with more opportunities, and we helped with the financial piece, but the latter alone would have been inadequate. Asad had learned to dream. The best part of that initial conversation? Asad was so stunned he forgot to make the delivery and arrived back at the restaurant with the food and an angry customer on the phone wondering why it sounded like a celebration on the other end of the line.

One of my favorite SNHU trustees often chafed at our discussions about equity and race, and argued that the best way for us to address those issues was to simply cut tuition and focus on making SNHU more affordable to more people. He would see Asad's story as confirmation of that theory, that Asad could be successful because we solved the financial barrier to access. Yet Asad's success—he went on to graduate with his bachelor's degree and stayed on for a master's degree— required more than financial aid. He had the vision of a better life that his experience at Foxborough had given him. He had people like Pops and others in his community, including his mother with all her struggles, rooting for him. He spent a number of holidays with my family, and we flew him to Oxford to join us there when visiting our daughter Emma (he often joked he was the Black son we never expected). Charismatic and likable, he readily made friends, and the campus community embraced him. People believed in him and that, in turn, helped him believe in himself. Even so, this wasn't enough.

Asad also had to be resilient. His mother came in and out of his life, bringing along all the emotional ups and downs that come with cycles of addiction and recovery. He was often hustling to make more money, doing sound and light production for events back in Boston. As a young Black man, he faced the constant calculus of navigating White culture, especially in New Hampshire, where every encounter could quickly become fraught. Like all of us moving across boundaries of class and community, he became a tweener, never again feeling fully at home in his old community nor having a sense of belonging in the new world he was navigating.

It was a feeling I had struggled with myself. I remember going into a high-stakes meeting during my time at Houghton Mifflin. The company's general counsel looked me up and down just before we entered the room and sniffed, "That's a bold choice of suit for this time of year." I had no idea what was wrong with my suit, but I knew I had made a mistake. It completely unnerved me, and I knew I didn't belong (I never hold grudges, but I think if I saw that guy today, I'd punch him). That was just a question of wardrobe, so imagine all the ways Asad had to overcome his own impostor syndrome, his feeling that he did not belong, all amplified by the racism that is baked into the everyday experiences of people of color. But Asad was resilient. He thrived at SNHU, built relationships, reached out to help others like him, and found community.

Not every story has such a happy ending, though. Sarah, which is not her real name, came to my attention when an SNHU alum and local high school principal named Pete came to see me about a senior who had been dealt an awful hand. She had no father, and her mother was both an addict and abusive. Sarah would take her little brother and spend all evening at a local pizza parlor, buying one slice and a soda to share. They would sit in a corner booth doing homework until closing time, with Sarah hoping her mother would be passed out when they got home because at least there would be peace in the house. Her teachers provided Sarah with hand-me-down clothes, often food, and sometimes a bit of money. While still in high school, she petitioned to become a ward of the state. Through all of this, she maintained a 3.6 grade point average. Pete said she would need a full scholarship from us—for books and everything else as well—and we said yes. I thought we had done the hard part with that yes, believing our financial commitment solved the issue. I was quickly to learn otherwise.

On the very first weekend, Sarah got into a spat with her new roommate and took a swing at her. The survival techniques of the street, where offense is often the best defense, especially for a young woman, were ill-suited for campus life. While SNHU's on-campus students are mostly from modest backgrounds, Sarah's bad dye jobs had made her hair damaged and unmanageable, and her clothes were unfashionable. She didn't fit in and knew it, and her resentment and anger, born of shame, bubbled just below the surface. Her boyfriend, someone in and out of the court system, would visit and cause trouble and was finally barred from campus. We had wrap-around services for her, but to no avail. We finally moved her into an alternative program that allowed her to live in her boyfriend's family home. We set her up with Laura, one of our most patient and compassionate staff members, someone who had deep experience working with challenging students like Sarah.

It got worse. Her story came to include heroin, pregnancy, dropping out, reenrolling, losing custody of her baby, detox, and a job—and a rollercoaster of emotions. Laura did everything, including being in the birthing room when the baby arrived and supplying Sarah with diapers, baby clothes, and equipment. Sarah would write to me from time to time, embarrassed that she "had let us down," apologetic and promising to get it together. They were the saddest letters of my career, too wrenching to share here.

Sarah's trauma was profound and internalized. She could *almost* imagine a better life for herself but self-sabotaged at every turn. And we did not recognize what she needed from us to be successful. It was a lesson I hadn't learned.

I've thought a lot about Sarah. We invested tens of thousands of dollars in her in terms of tuition and more. I personally monitored her situation, but what I did not do was give her my time or my attention. I can justify that in terms of my busy job and my role—no one would have expected me to do more than I did—and if people knew that I quietly wrote a personal check to cover the cost of baby clothes and diapers, they might even applaud me for my care. But writing a check is not time. It was the easy way out and required no emotional investment on my part. As Matt Steinfeld said, helping Sarah required holding the space of her trauma and being emotionally available to her. I had done neither.

With Asad, I had given him my time and my care, and I have thought a lot about why. I think it was because Asad was easier. He was charismatic, already had aspirations—we shared some interests—and was widely liked. None of that was true for Sarah. I think I failed Sarah because the task of doing otherwise was too hard, something I'm a little ashamed to admit. It takes a lot to hold the space of people who have so much trauma, who live such different lives, who move through the world in ways that can even be distasteful. Writing a check for Sarah was not fundamentally different from the act of a rich parent who lavishes material objects on a child but provides neither time nor emotional connection. It missed the point.

What made the difference for Sarah and Asad? I go back to what Matt Biel said about the three conditions necessary for a person to have resilience: a passion for something, someone who believes in them, and a sustained period of a better or more normal life that they can hold on to and imagine for themselves.

Sarah had no discernible passion. She did have people who believed in her (Laura even considered legally adopting her), but her emotional defenses were too stout to ever fully accept their support. And she had never known a truly good year. Her deadbeat boyfriend offered the closest thing to love she knew, and getting pregnant when she knew better only seemed to confirm the narrative she felt the world had written for her. Her baby was the sole light in her life, and when we last conversed, she had been sober for months, was working, and hoping to regain custody. Will we ever get her across the finish line with a degree? Our very large population of nontraditional learners, most of whom follow indirect paths to their degrees, tells me it is possible. Perhaps the odds are just too stacked against her. My hope is that having a daughter will impel her to a better vision for her child's life; that we can convince her to believe in herself (she is so smart that she is more than capable of the work); and that she can muster the necessary resilience when she is faced with the inevitable headwinds. When I ask our online graduates why they came back to complete a degree, they often say "for my kids." Perhaps for Sarah, imagining a better life for her daughter will be the dream that gets her back in school someday.

Asad had all three components of resiliency and hope. He had a passion for his sound and light work and dreamed of owning his own business. He had a large number of people who believed in him, and he embraced their conviction and internalized it. Plus he had his years at Foxborough High, when he had the support of Pops, a place to stay, and a vision of what a good school experience could be. He had Matt's three critical components to hold on to his dreams and aspirations when he faced headwinds.

We chatted recently—his sound-and-lighting business survived the pandemic—and he is hoping to buy a home. He is realizing his dream. There are many more challenging Sarahs out there than the exceptional Asads, and our challenge is to help them dream bigger dreams for themselves. But that work starts with us as individuals and requires systems that measure their success by the lives they change and that are built to give us all the time, space, and resources to be successful. In short, it requires systems that combat the self-serving dynamics of serving people at scale.

THE POWER OF STORIES

In my Acadian household, stories were the social currency of any gathering. Not political debates, reviews of the latest novel or movie, plans for travel—those were not part of our discourse. At family gatherings when I was a kid, we always waited for the best storytellers, my uncle Wilfred or my sister Betty Ann, to take their turn. Wilfred, with a bushy eighteenth-century mustache and mischievously twinkling blue eyes, could with a knowing glance or raised eyebrow make even a young kid like me feel like the story being told at the table was really only for me and not the others. Betty Ann's stories always had a tinge of outrage, taking on some bureaucrat or person in power, but always with self-deprecating humor and a salty word or two. There were the known embellishers, acknowledged through the shared glances and wry smiles of others as they told a story a little more dramatic and less plausible than the times they had told it before. Laughter coursed through these rounds of storytelling, which were mostly about getting by, overcoming obstacles, and never taking the world or oneself too seriously. Telling stories was our best tool for resiliency, and these stories were so often about just that.

I remember being on a business trip when I heard that Uncle Wilfred had received a terrible medical diagnosis. He had woken up one morning to discover an eye nearly swollen shut. At the emergency room, the attending physician asked him about his last physical. "I haven't had one." Thinking that Wilfred, now in his seventies, might have misheard, the doctor said, "No, I mean when was the last time you saw your doctor for a physical exam or any issue." Wilfred's answer was the same. He had never seen a doctor in over seven decades of farming and construction work. The astonished doctor quickly established that the swollen eye was from a spider bite, ordered an antihistamine to reduce the swelling, and took the occasion to do a routine physical and order some basic baseline lab work.

The results were not good. Wilfred, a lifelong heavy smoker, had advanced lung cancer. The doctor brought in an oncologist, and they talked through the treatment options and their recommendations for how to proceed. Wilfred listened patiently; thanked them; said, "I'm going to pass on the treatments"; and walked out.

When I returned from my trip, I drove to his house, where I found him sitting in a lawn chair, smoking a cigarette, and watering his tomato plants. He seemed very much his old self. We chatted, and I broached the subject of his cancer diagnosis. He shared that his cancer was quite advanced, the treatments aggressive, and that he had decided against any of it. I gently asked if he might at least get a second opinion. He looked at me, blue eyes still twinkling, and said in a deadpan, "Paul, I didn't like the first opinion much. I don't think I want another." He spent the summer in his garden, smoked a lot of cigarettes, and had a mostly painless and gracious passing that fall.

While I was growing up, all the family stories were retold again and again, which strained my patience when I reached adolescence and had heard them, oh, hundreds of times, but I later understood better. The stories affirmed our values and constructed our sense of the world, a world where hardship was expected, hard work respected, rewards modest, and putting one over on those in power celebrated. When a bottle of Seagrams 7 whiskey—or Crown Royal if someone was feeling flush—sat at the center of the table, the stories became a bit more ribald, so kids were shooed off to bed or to play in another room, while mothers shared in the laughter and contributed their own commentary. I learned to tell stories at those gatherings and at some point was expected to have a story to tell. It's how we honed our craft.

The ability to tell a good story would come to serve me well. I was delighted to recently learn that Netflix's cofounder Reed Hastings and I shared an adolescent job: we both sold vacuum cleaners. We went door-to-door, cold-calling on people to persuade them to buy an Electrolux vacuum cleaner. Hastings liked the work so much that he deferred his admission to Bowdoin College to continue the job for another year. He later described what he had liked about it—meeting people and telling stories—which was the same reason I enjoyed the work. I discovered I could sell vacuums pretty well and made a lot of money that one summer.

Likewise, I won a trip to Washington, DC, by selling subscriptions to the *Boston Herald*. As with telling stories around the family table, I learned that selling is most successful when the opening captures the listener's attention, when the pitch has an arc, when evidence makes the story authentic (in my case, actually dumping a small bag of ash on the whitest carpet I could find in the customer's house), and when the end surprises and satisfies (as when the carpet's condition is quickly restored and not a trace of ash could be found). I also learned that good storytellers know when to stop and when to listen and can only be effective if they connect with the other listener in some very human way.

I went off to college and entered a world much different from the one in which I grew up, so stories were harder for me to tell when I came home. And because my new stories were not of the shared experiences and values of my clan, they often fell flat and set me apart. In retrospect, my guess is that they elicited some combination of pride, wonderment, and disapproval—the last because my stories distinguished me from my family rather than affirmed my belonging. The first piece of writing I ever published was in my college literary magazine, a short story called "The Easy Life" in which I described a working-class kid coming home from college and realizing the ways he no longer fits in.

Stories in my family, as in organizations, held us together in a shared sense of ourselves and the world. That kind of myth making is powerful. The collective story asserts values, affirms or condemns behaviors, and provides an aspirational standard to which all are judged. Because it is bound up in our sense of honor and how we want others to perceive us, we often leave out the stories that are no less true but mostly unwanted.

Families are full of stories that are taken to the grave or only whispered among the few who know "the real truth." I had an older cousin (so much older I called him my uncle) whom I always looked forward to seeing. He was funny, drove cooler cars than the others, and was an excellent hockey player (the highest virtue in my Canadian family). Only recently did my sister Betty Ann share with me that he was almost certainly sexually abusing a daughter, which is almost impossible for me to write (I worry about the disapproval of my family should they ever read these words). Every remembered interaction with him is now cast through a different lens.

When my sister shared this dark side of our cousin, long ago deceased, I realized that while all the things I thought of him were true, there was another set of facts I either willfully disregarded or ignored through a kind of confirmation bias. There was the petty thievery, the rumors of him "playing around," the dirty jokes not quite age appropriate for us, the acts of slipping us beer when we were still underage, and the apparent and coarse libido that then seemed cool in a slightly bad boy sort of way to adolescent young cousins trying to understand manhood.

We were constructing a story about him, disregarding the facts that did not quite fit. I now think we suspected that story was inauthentic, but we liked the parts that we liked too much to make room for the uncomfortable. If there had been sexual abuse, I am pretty sure no one in our family knew it—that would be such a gross violation of values that no one would simply choose to ignore it. But to discover that there likely was abuse points out to me the way all stories include and leave out what we need in order to find authenticity. When we leave out big parts of the story, either intentionally or unintentionally, as we did with my cousin, the story we do tell becomes inauthentic and a kind of lie that goes beyond a mere faithful rendering of the details.

When I first became a college president, this tension between the stories we tell and the stories we know but don't tell became a problem for me. There is an old joke that college presidents live in big houses and beg for money. Raising money for one's institution is a critical part of the job for most college and university presidents, and when I arrived at Marlboro College in 1996, I discovered I was pretty good at it. Fundraising is really storytelling, constructing stories that inspire and move an audience to write a check. When I sat down with the Smiths (not their real name), I told a compelling story that I hoped would end with them writing a check to build a new music and dance building on campus. Marlboro had a vibrant dance program, an excellent music program, and was the summer home of the famous Marlboro Music Festival. While the festival, founded by luminaries Rudolf Serkin, Adolf Busch, and Pablo Casals, was not a part of the college and simply rented the campus, it inextricably bound the college's reputation with music.

Here was a chance for the Smiths to build a dedicated music and dance building designed by a famous architect with modern rehearsal studios, an acoustically rich performance hall, a dance space with a spring floor, and recording facilities. I was able to share how the current spaces we had were worn out and inadequate, how our students struggled to rehearse and perform so were relegated to a theater designed for neither dance nor music. I told the stories of actual students, using their real names and explaining why the Smiths would like them, then related how they struggled against some limitation of our space. I knew the Smiths to be modest and mostly self-made people, able to give the millions required to build the facility but inexperienced with giving at that level. They were almost surprised that we could be talking about such a large gift and that they had reached a place in life where they could give it.

I unrolled the architect's blueprint of the building, explained each room and function it performed, and patiently answered their questions. Then I presented drawings of what the building would actually look like from different angles, finishing with the final page, a rendering of the main entrance complete with student figures going in and out of the building. Best of all, the rendering included their names over the entrance, placed there for all of posterity. I saw their expressions brighten and the exchange of glances that signaled they were hooked. I left so they could have the private conversation they now needed, the one in which they reassured themselves they could afford to make this gift and could exclaim over the beauty of the building, reciting the needs it would fill for our students—all of that masking their real but unspoken delight at having their names there for everyone to see, letters on the side of a building that said they matter.

Like all great stories, it started with a noble goal: to help talented young students, dancers, and musicians realize their dreams. It included the mandatory struggles, which in this case were the poor facilities that held back those deserving young people. The Smiths could be the heroes of the story, wielding the weapon that heroes always must—in this case, their wealth. Like the best heroes, their roots were humble, their intentions good, and they would come to the rescue with humility and grace.

We are hardwired for such stories, and those basic elements extend from second-century BC *Gilgamesh* to today's Harry Potter series. When such stories work, we empathize and see ourselves in the hero. My job that day was to help the Smiths see themselves as the heroes of the story I told. I had been having such meetings with donors for over six years at that point and knew when to bow out, saying something about being grateful for their time, their needing to talk to their accountant, and insisting that the blueprints were an extra copy for them to keep. I was that confident of the gift.

As I drove away, I also knew I had to leave my job at Marlboro.

Storytelling as Knowing

I had to leave because I could no longer tell a true story of the college, robbing me of the single most important tool of a leader. In so much of the literature on organizations, storytelling is relegated to marketing, brand building, and internal communications. Those functions are all important and part of organizational storytelling, but they are often framed as the stories we tell after the core work is completed. And, as such, the literature misses a much bigger point: stories—the ones we tell and the ones we collect—are the single most powerful tool we have as leaders. Stories are how we think. They do not come after the work; they are the work. E. O. Wilson, the famous sociobiologist, says:

Human beings are the storytelling species. The way we think is in narrative. We build scenarios forward and when we are making a decision, we are running one scenario after another forward. We are telling a story to ourselves. "I'm going to do this and that will follow and so and so will probably do this and so on. And I will lose that or I'll gain this or I will finish that." And they tell stories of the real past, what happened to me. Of course, this allows them to make fictional stories. The scientist tells stories and he hopes they will be true stories . . . These are called hypotheses and the fancy term for doing science by storytelling is the method of multiple competing hypotheses. You do the experiments to see which of the stories is true.[1]

Storytelling is not a thing we sometimes do. It is the way we navigate the world minute by minute with a story always running and evolving inside our head, constructing reality about ourselves, about others, and about the world as we imagine it, because the world is inherently a construct of our imagination. Or as Jonathan Gottschall, author of *The Storytelling Animal: How Stories Make Us Human*, says:

> You might not realize it, but you are a creature of an imaginative realm called Neverland. Neverland is your home, and before you die, you will spend decades there. If you haven't noticed this before, don't despair: story is for a human as water is for a fish— all-encompassing and not quite palpable. While your body is always fixed at a particular point in space-time, your mind is always free to ramble in lands of make-believe. And it does.[2]

When we are at our best as thinkers, we are testing our Neverland stories against evidence. We might ask what the data tells us about our outcomes as an organization, for example. And when I was distracted by my phone as my ten-year-old was telling me about school, was I the good parent I liked to tell myself I was? What am I ignoring right now because it tells a story that makes me uncomfortable? When we don't like the answer, we can rationalize (I was only on the phone for a minute), or we can use the evidence to see the gaps in the stories we tell about ourselves and then improve.

When Lorris Betz started his work to improve the University of Utah Health system, one of the first things he discovered was that patient complaint letters were routinely collected, but they never made their way to him. He was only hearing the good stories. He insisted on seeing the letters, and they confirmed what he feared—that patients were often experiencing the health-care system in ways far different from those the system was telling itself. Those unhappy stories helped fuel his work to improve the health-care system he led. Lorris made videos out of the most troubling stories and showed them to doctors, nurses, and other staff so they could once again see the real people they were serving (often poorly) and understand the real consequences of forgetting their needs. He says they still make him cry when he sees them.

So the question we must ask as leaders of large organizations or systems is, "How are we hearing from the least among us, from the least well served, from those with the least frequent opportunity to tell a story?" We need to collect all of the stories to test the story we most often tell.

In a recent meeting of some two hundred of SNHU's managers and supervisors, we shared the recording of employees talking about not being able to show up at work as their full selves, being in meetings where they felt they had to assume a role that was more accepted, and being afraid to speak their minds. I could sense the discomfort in the room, and I, too, was skeptical about some of what I heard. It would have been easy for me to say, "But that's so-and-so and they are always complaining" or "Why does she think anyone would care if she shared that she is . . . ," but I forced myself to stay open to the truths that might be in those stories. I like to tell the story of how SNHU is getting better in terms of inclusivity, and from my vantage point, I can see the truth in that story. But my vantage point, lofty as it is, is limited because it is not immersed in all of the day-to-day meetings of frontline staff. The stories I heard in that meeting, even if only partially accurate, reflected the ways those nine employees experienced our organization. They might conclude, as I uncomfortably did, that the story I was telling about inclusivity is not yet true. Hearing all the stories, not just the ones that confirm our mythmaking, is the only way to get better as an organization.

In Lorris's health-care system, a tremendous amount of good work was going on, lives were being saved, and medical professionals were telling themselves a reassuring story about how good they were. But that single story would have provided an incomplete truth. In uncovering and sharing the unhappy stories, Lorris was presenting not an alternative narrative, but an additional story. When taken together, he could then have a more complete story of the University of Utah Health system and know where it could improve. Similarly, our managers who were squirming a bit in their chairs had been working hard to be more inclusive and to empower their people. We have made a lot of progress, but we have a lot more work to do. Both things can be true. Both stories can resonate.

In a wonderful TEDGlobal talk from 2009, the writer Chimamanda Adiche talks about the danger of a single story. Having been raised on beloved books by British and American writers, it was only later that she discovered books by African writers like Chinua Achebe and Camara Laye. She says:

Now, I loved those American and British books I read. They stirred my imagination. They opened up new worlds for me. But the unintended consequence was that I did not know that people like me could exist in literature. So what the discovery of African writers did for me was this: it saved me from having a single story of what books are.[3]

When we tell a single story, our thinking is incomplete, the reality we construct less true. When we do that with people, we risk the dehumanization that characterizes so many of our systems in America. As Adiche says:

I've always felt that it is impossible to engage properly with a place or a person without engaging all the stories of that place and person. The consequence of the single story is this: it robs people of dignity. It makes our recognition of our equal humanity difficult. It emphasizes how we are different rather than how we are similar.[4]

Adiche's observation echoes Ken Oliver's description of the single story correctional officers are given: that all inmates are beneath contempt and to be treated as such.

Woody Holton, the University of South Carolina historian and scholar of the American Revolution, was asked what would happen if people could hold multiple stories in hand at the same time and replied:

George Floyd would be alive. I think it would have that kind of impact, that if people could think in a broader way, it would really not eliminate but put a real dent in things like racism and misogyny, because what they're really founded on is the principle that there's us good guys—hey, we're the Minneapolis cops. We're out here fighting for law and order. And then there's these criminals who we don't have to respect the lives of. If we could get out of black hats and white hats, the impact on society would be immeasurably positive.[5]

If we are to improve systems and make them more human centered, we have to listen to all the stories we can even when that is uncomfortable.

In 2009, I was six years into my presidency at SNHU, and things were going really well. We were growing, revenues were healthy, and we were establishing ourselves as a leader in online education. The plan was working, and I was getting praise from the board of trustees and outsiders who were watching this small, unknown local institution suddenly getting everyone's attention. Ironically, I was worried, fearing that success and accolades might be blinding me to stories I was not hearing. So I asked twelve of my fiercest critics on the faculty to join me for dinner and tell me what I was doing wrong. The invitation read:

> Now this will feel like a bit of an unorthodox invitation, but I was hoping you might be willing to join me for dinner and a discussion about the state of the university. I'd also like to share some thoughts I have around the strategic plan and questions I've been grappling with as we look out ahead over the next five to ten years.
>
> The unorthodox part, as you review the list of invitees, is that I wanted to bring together those who fall into one or more of the following categories:
>
> 1. Those who really think I am taking the place down the wrong road or have a very different vision of where we should go
> 2. Those who have been critical of one or more initiatives in the past or currently underway
> 3. Those who have not been shy about speaking up and who I believe will speak their minds in the discussion I hope to have

4. Those who just straight out don't like me
5. Those who by virtue of their elected or appointed position represent faculty in some important capacity

I've included you because I think you likely fall into one or more of the categories. You can place yourself in whatever categories that feel most accurate or comfortable (perhaps all!). As you scan the list, you are also people who have years of experience here, have been leaders in one way or another, and who think and care deeply about the place (even if we disagree from time to time or all the time).

It's very easy to find a group of people who will tell me they like what we are doing and who will heap praise, but I'd welcome a discussion with those who might strongly disagree with those notions.

I look forward to your response.

Paul

I arranged for a private room at a local restaurant, had all the food and drinks brought in, and asked the servers to close the door and leave us undisturbed. No one sat near me as we took our seats, and conversation was at first awkward and slow. I stuck with my resolve to remain largely quiet, ask clarifying questions, and take notes.

As one attendee later noted, the setting felt like neutral territory, and once they warmed up, the criticisms readily came forward, often with some emotional heat. As one commented, "you could see the steam curling from their ears." For example, they unanimously objected to a new marketing campaign and its "Go the extra mile" slogan. One person called it ghastly and said it "just made people want to commit suicide." I could feel my face reddening, and it took all my willpower not to call out the hyperbole, point out flaws in arguments, or defend decisions, but I instead listened to their comments as a kind of unfolding counternarrative, a story quite different from the one I was telling myself and others about the work of the university. Some of it was painful because it felt personal and ungracious and I have a last-born's need to be liked, but I reminded myself to take deep breaths. I nodded and kept taking notes, and finally thanked them for their candor and promised to think deeply about what they had shared.

A number of them later reported that their own views had changed and that they felt heard. More importantly, I had to admit that some of what they said that evening was true. The story I was telling myself wasn't entirely accurate. What I saw at the table actually reaffirmed most of what we were doing. My critics were not entirely wrong, and I knew my team and I had to fix some things.

Paul Fain, a reporter at the *Chronicle of Higher Education* at the time, heard me tell this story at a conference and wrote an article about it. He later told me it was the second most forwarded article in the *Chronicle* that year, perhaps speaking to a need for people across our industry to have their stories heard more often.[6]

As leaders, we need to test our narratives all the time, probing for facts that will complete the stories we tell ourselves or others. As systems start to dehumanize the people they serve, there are numerous ways in which the uncomfortable stories get suppressed, the counterfactual is held at bay, and complex human stories get reduced and two-dimensional. It can be managers and supervisors wanting to only present a rosy picture. It can be a sense that presenting uncomfortable truths will be punished or resented, threatening opportunities for advancement or even one's job. It can also be that we like the benefits we enjoy in the status quo and an alternative story might risk those advantages. Sometimes we just don't like what those additional stories tell us about ourselves.

The Power of the Uncomfortable Story

There is great power in uncovering the uncomfortable truths when we need to change our organizations or ourselves. Like Lorris at the University of Utah Health, I have been trying to calibrate our need to impact and serve more students with the creeping dehumanization of bureaucracy I sense in an organization as large as SNHU. I still often tell the stories of our successful students, inspiring stories of grit and perseverance and our people doing the right things to help those students graduate. However, I am now increasingly seeking out the stories of our failures as well. For example, I remind people that our small campus of three thousand students now has only 6 percent first-generation students, as our tuition has put those programs out of financial reach for many. I remind them that we like to say that we are the college for working-class kids and first-generation students, yet the facts are now making that narrative less authentic.

We have an employee engagement platform called Peakon, which allows employees to anonymously respond to a series of questions. I sometimes pull stories from Peakon to highlight what I call warning flags. In one division, where we like to say we empower our teams, there was feedback that people didn't even have time to get a bathroom break. Not very empowering. Other stories captured a kind of time clock mentality, contradicting the story we were telling ourselves about our work culture.

Our system needs, goal setting, and data collection were beginning to supersede our care for our people—creeping dehumanization. Those stories drove changes in leadership within that division, but that tension between the system's demands and our focus on doing the right thing for people sits in a kind of unresolved tension that we are working on still.

Similarly, three years ago I found myself telling my wife, Pat, that things were going so well at work that I felt I had really mastered my role, that I rarely saw issues or problems that I hadn't seen before and couldn't sort out, and that as an organization we were really firing on all cylinders. (I am still Catholic enough to have known better to give in to such self-satisfaction.)

At the time, we were using an outside consultant to access the integration of a recently acquired organization. He spent some weeks on the assignment, but one day asked if he could meet with Amelia Manning, my longtime chief operating officer and right-hand person, and me on another topic "out of scope," as he said. He needed ninety minutes. When we met, he praised our leadership, described the respect our people had for us, and echoed much of what I had confidently shared with Pat. Then he dropped the bomb. He said, "You are not creating leaders here at SNHU. Everyone defers to you, asks 'What do Amelia and Paul want us to do?' and you are not making them better." He shared painful examples, and in that moment, I knew he was telling a true story. It was devastating. I wasn't at the top of my game. Indeed, if one definition of a leader is "someone who creates leaders," I was failing miserably. I immediately rewrote his contract and asked him to interview everyone on the leadership team and present to the whole group with no preview for me.

When we met as a group just a few weeks later, we had a very tough meeting. I had to hear uncomfortable stories and truths. At the very moment that it seemed I was the sole focus of the problem, he turned to my team and told them they lacked courage, comfortably delegated up to Amelia and me, and were not the leaders their people needed them to be. It was not one of those meetings where we broke glass and then worked toward resolution. We all left that meeting feeling beaten up, unclear about next steps, and pained.

We scheduled a two-day retreat for just a couple of weeks later and had an extraordinary meeting, agreeing on how we would work going forward. We talked about moving away from our command-and-control approach, building a learning culture, and stepping away from our expert silos to a more collaborative and inquisitive form of leadership.

We continue to work at it—some days we are better at it than others—but it is a story in draft form, and we wouldn't be writing it if the story I was telling myself had not been challenged. We had to come to grips with a truer story of ourselves in order to write a different next chapter.

In our early days, leading what was still a modest-size organization at the time, it was easy for me to keep an ear to the ground, know my harshest critics, and pull together a dinner such as the one described earlier. Now, operating at scale and with thousands of employees spread across the country, the majority working remotely, it is much harder to collect those alternative stories. There are tools that help, like Peakon, a platform that allows employees to give anonymous feedback. We also do Voice of the Customer (we use Voice of the Student in our context) research to better understand the students we serve and how we can improve by using surveys and focus groups and other methods to collect student feedback. That helps, but genuine listening takes time and presence.

Before the pandemic, my work increasingly took me away, often telling SNHU's story to others. When the pandemic stopped that travel, I used my newfound time to do more listening sessions with teams across the university, and I describe those as the great gift of the pandemic to me professionally. I started collecting stories in a way I hadn't in a long time. Mostly I just asked questions and listened. As people got more comfortable, they would sometimes answer my questions of where we are dropping the ball and where we can be better with more candor. Often I disagreed with their analysis, but because of that dinner many years ago now, I had trained myself to listen carefully and probe for the portions that might be true.

I also sought out people I knew to be student centered and mission focused, and asked them the same questions. That was sometimes painful. One said of a reorganization effort on campus, "In all my years at SNHU it was the first time I felt like I was being moved around like the boxes in my garage, with no one asking me what I thought we should do." I got off that video call and reflected on the signals I had been ignoring around the reorganization, and asked why. I think I didn't want to believe it had been going off the tracks and that the unhappy voices were simply malcontents or the inherent by-product of change. They were neither. We had mismanaged the process, so I hit the pause button, brought in an expert to take stock of the work, shared that with everyone, and followed up with a ten-day listening period to gather people's responses. I also resolved to be at work more so I could hear the stories—and also tell the stories of why we were doing this hard thing, a narrative that had been lost in the unhappiness. At the time of this writing, the work continues.

The Power of the Affirming Story

While it is the job of leaders to collect stories, to accept no single story, and to know the stories of those they serve, they are also called upon to tell stories. Indeed, it is often said that the leader of an organization is its storyteller-in-chief. Leaders are called upon to tell the story of the organization they lead within the organization and also to external audiences, and in those stories are the values, the mission, and the vision of their organization.

Within their organization, leaders are the keepers of lore with all its heroes and villains, hard times and glories, symbols and myth making.

All systems and organizations are in the business of storytelling in part because even in this data-obsessed age, when technology and scale are canonized, there's far more power to motivate and move people through stories than there is through data. Yes, the old axiom advises, "No stories without data and no data without stories," but it offers a false equivalency. Stories are far more powerful than data, and good storytelling can act as a rehumanizing counterbalance that touches the heart in a way that data never does.

While data often fails to move people, stories can make the world take notice. *New York Times* columnist Nicholas Kristof defends his storytelling about individuals, saying that humans don't really process large numbers and, for example, can be emotionally unmoved by data documenting millions of people starving to death. But one story or picture—say of Kevin Carter's 1993 Pulitzer Prize–winning photo of a collapsed starving child with a vulture patiently waiting in the background during the famine in South Sudan—can touch people deeply, prompting them to call for intervention and rescue. Such stories elicit empathy. The necessary first step in getting people to fix broken systems is for them to start caring for the people those systems serve, know their stories, and connect in a very human way.

Dennis Littky, the founder of the Met and College Unbound, whom we met in a previous chapter, is a gifted educator and storyteller. He knows the power of stories we tell internally, to the people who work within organizations. He says:

> The other thing is that when you talk about what's really important, when you want to reinforce culture and make sure people understand the values of what you are building, the stories tell everything. When somebody says, "Hey, the whole advisory got on a bus and went to Jean's house because she wasn't coming to

school and pulled her back"—all of a sudden that tells them that you got to do whatever you got to do to get a kid back. Stories play a very important role in passing on and reinforcing culture. A handbook doesn't do it. A book written about it doesn't do it. But people remember what somebody did. That's important.

Alexander Packard, the former president of the nationwide Iora Health system and current chief integration officer since its 2021 acquisition by One Medical, echoes those ideas when he says storytelling is a huge part of the company's culture. When I talked with him, he was preparing to attend a meeting with 750 employees that would start with a story:

> A health coach from one of our practices . . . is going to tell a story about a patient who was incredibly hard to reach psychologically. They felt like she just wasn't engaging. Fast forward through the story—they found out that there was a really profound life issue going on for this patient. Only once they could make that topic discussable did this patient truly engage, and then she really engaged. She had a lot going on, and she allowed us to help her . . . I think the power of stories is incredibly profound. We often tell patient stories because we know that it increases the amount of pride that people have in their work, that our organization is doing this. But there's also a teachable moment in each one. The teachable moment in today's story is being persistent with a patient and knowing that if you continue to build trust and you show up for them, that ultimately—you don't know when—that barrier will come down emotionally, their vulnerability, and that that's when we can really help patients.

What Lorris, Dennis, and Alexander recognize is that while leaders are often their organizations' storytellers-in-chief, it is often more powerful to let the people working within or served by their organizations do the telling. In that sense, they know leaders can play an important role not just in the stories they tell, but also in collecting stories and providing a stage or platform for their protagonists to tell their own stories. Those choices of whose stories we share, what stories we tell, and what stories we are willing to hear raise questions of authenticity and truth.

When I had to acknowledge some uncomfortable realities in that dinner conversation with faculty, I realized that the story of institutional change I was telling was not entirely true. My subsequent storytelling inside SNHU more often included a recognition that the changes we were doing were hard and not always on target or embraced by all. I also realized that the story I was telling did not allow space for the stories of other important stakeholders.

In a sense, telling incomplete stories or single stories, as Adiche warns us, is an exercise of power that can dehumanize the people about which those stories are told. I worked for three years heading a new technology group for a large publishing firm, and in management team meetings I often heard joking or disparaging remarks about faculty, the customers for their textbooks and other products. Finally, I spoke up and asked, "Does it bother anyone else that we are always making fun of faculty, our customers, and the authors of the textbooks that are the source of all our revenue?" The room went silent and then there were halfhearted attempts to explain that "it was joking around" and "we don't really mean it." Later that day, the head of the division pulled me aside and said she had not realized how that attitude had crept into the team's discourse and that if we hadn't named it and stopped it, it would have started to change how we treated the very people we were serving and with whom we often partnered.

The inverse can also be true—we can tell stories that lift others up. If you own a television and live in America, you've likely seen an SNHU commercial. While many other universities advertise in some manner, they most often talk about themselves and often in terms of status: how much research they produce, their winning teams, the Nobel Prize winner on their faculty, and the beauty of their campus. We instead tell the stories of our students and invite our prospective students to see themselves in those stories. That is why we so often feature graduation with real graduates who represent the diversity of those we educate, often surrounded by loved ones. We are saying that college can be part of your story, too.

For too many people, the stories they have for themselves are the internalized stories others have told about them. Emily McCann, former CEO of Citizen Schools, explains:

> Often, kids' narratives about themselves are defined by other people. They don't necessarily know who they are, particularly as they are coming into middle school. They know they are defined by their parents. "My mom says I'm XYZ. My teacher says I'm XYZ. My brother says I'm XYZ." And they are trying to negotiate their own space within that narrative assigned to them, trying to understand themselves. When you hear a kid say, "I'm an astronaut. I'm a scientist," you recognize that they are telling you something about themselves that nobody else has defined, certainly not the dominant adults in their lives. When kids were beginning to share that narrative themselves and beginning to tell the stories of their experiences in our program, we knew we were onto something big.

For our students at SNHU, the stories they often tell about themselves are ones of struggle, failure, and self-doubt. Sara Goldrick-Rab comments:

In those moments, I ask, "Do you know how many other students are in exactly the same boat? How mathematical would it be that all of you made the same exact set of bad decisions?" I help them see the structure. Then I say, "The system wants you to give up. Think about who wins when you give up. So you, Black woman, you don't get a degree. You don't get to raise your family up. You don't get these things. So you stay exactly where people want you." There's a huge turnaround. When they get it, they start to fight the system, and they want to beat the system. Now we have this thing, which becomes this empowered "I'm going to do this so that the system doesn't beat me."

Sara helps them rethink the story they tell about themselves as a first critical step in helping them write the next chapter in their life story. When Arne Duncan does something similar with the young men with whom he works in the Chicago CRED programs, he is affirming that finding the truth in our own stories is critical to writing whatever chapters come next. He insists that the men with whom he works revisit the stories they have told about themselves before they go on to the stories they want to tell in the future.

I tell a story of my days at Marlboro that Marlboro never tells. In my version, I am the hero of my story, the young president (thirty-nine was young for a college president) who took a place on the verge of collapse and turned it around, raising millions of dollars, renewing the campus infrastructure (starting on week one with a failing septic system and a threat of closure), getting national media attention, creating new sources of revenue, and raising long-stagnant salaries. Yet in the histories of Marlboro, I figure not at all and was invited back just once. If Marlboro were still around (it closed in 2020), the story I think it would have told would be of a young leader who didn't listen hard enough, who did not tell the stories of which Marlboro was most proud, who showed a palpable disdain for the rustic facilities that some long-serving staff had actually built themselves, and who quickly dismissed dissent as mere truculence. I did not honor Marlboro's stories, and, in turn, it never honored mine. When a leader tells a story that feels out of alignment with people's lived reality—no matter whose version of reality is considered more true—it often means time for a change of the kind I made after my meeting with the Marlboro donors.

Of course, as leaders we are often writing the next chapter for our organization and have to tell a story that is more aspirational than current reality. In his novel *Mother Night*, Kurt Vonnegut writes, "We are what we pretend to be, so we must be careful what we pretend to be."[7] When we shine a light on the behaviors we most want to see in our organizations, even when they might not be as common as we would like, we are asking those who fall short to aspire, in essence to pretend they are as good as those colleagues being highlighted, because they are more likely to actually get that good.

As we seek to innovate at SNHU, we often say we recognize and embrace learning wherever it happens. That's more aspirational than true right now, as our systems make that reality difficult to achieve, but in saying it over and over again, our organization rallies behind the aspirational, and I am convinced that we will become what we pretend to be in this case. Am I telling an untrue story? Truth is not black and white or a single story. It requires me to hold at once all the stories I love to tell about how good we are and what we do for our students, the stories that make me cringe and include ways that we fail the people we want to serve, and the stories that are not yet quite true but that we are working to make authentic.

Rediscovering the Stories of Those We Serve

There is much in our world that reduces and simplifies our stories. Scale and efficiency drive organizations and systems to categorize and label people. Data analytics has taken that tendency to new heights, with predictive analysis now shaping the kinds of information we receive. For example, Facebook feeds its users more news and information that conforms to what the algorithm predicts they want to see, whether true or not. Algorithmic profiling often reinforces bias and reduces our understanding of the world and ourselves, dehumanizing others while simplifying and reinforcing the stories we tell about ourselves.

We all walk around with a story we tell about ourselves and narratives for all those with whom we interact. When those stories get overly simplified, when they lose the complexity of individual human stories, it becomes so much easier to valorize one's own ideology while demonizing the "other." It gives us the "Big Lie" of the 2020 election, the storming of the Capitol, and sows the seeds of nationalism and even genocide.

The loss of story and the dehumanization that comes with it are often driven by more mundane factors. If a system is underfunded, such as much of public K–12 education, or faces quarterly pressure to eke out every penny of profit to increase shareholder value, there is even greater pressure to reduce individual human complexity to categories with standardized and efficient (less expensive) responses that are perhaps less effective. What gets lost in that dynamic is a deeper understanding of the individuals we serve and the complexity that is any human life. In other words, not knowing the multiple stories of those being served is seeing them as being less fully human.

In her book *Manifesto for a Moral Revolution*, Jacqueline Novogratz, the noted founder of Acumen, a social impact nonprofit that fights global poverty, recalls a meeting in Pakistan in which she suggested that Nobel Prize winner Malala Yousafzi exemplified moral leadership. While half the room readily agreed, she received unexpected dissent, and one young man from Swat, Malala's home region, said, "Malala is no hero of mine. Her story has been manipulated to make the West feel good about itself." He went on to explain how Swat had been a progressive place, educating girls, how the Taliban had punished them for doing so, and how he and others in his community were reduced to the role of barbarians in the stories told about Malala's genuine heroism. In fact, as Novogratz writes, he led a school for both boys and girls, fought to protect girls' education, and was an educated and proud Pakistani from the reviled northern territories.[8] In that conversation gone wrong, Novogratz asked people to let him tell his story and she writes:

> If we had not had time as a group to consider the complexities of this man's life experiences and the story of Malala herself, we could have become even more divided. Instead, we deliberately created space and time for uncomfortable conversations among people who, above all else, valued listening and moral imagination.[9]

She summarizes:

> At the essence of the Malala exchange was the interplay of human dignity and identity; a yearning to be recognized and acknowledged; an unspoken promise: if you do not attempt to reduce me to a single identity, I will try to see you as a more integrated person as well.[10]

If we are to build systems that put people at the center of the work, we have to build systems that understand people's stories in their complexity; in other words, systems that see people as fully human, complex, possessing multiple stories, and not easily categorized.

It is easy to suggest that scaled systems and organizations simply cannot understand individuals in the ways just described, but Alexander Packard is building a health-care system that does just that and proclaims it as its tagline: "restoring humanity to health care." At the heart of the approach is its use of health coaches, whose work is to bridge the distance between the busy physician and the patient. Similar to our use of academic coaches at SNHU or Groups Recover Together's use of counselors in the lead care role, One Medical's health coaches get to know their patients in the fullness of their individual lives. As he explains:

The health coach's job is to really understand the life circumstances, the well-being of the patient. Who lives at home with them? What are their hopes and dreams? Where are their barriers and obstacles? What's going on in their lives? The abusive relationship, the addiction, the stress, the fact that they just got fired or their spouse is cheating or whatever's going on in their life. That actually plays a huge role in our well-being. The classic doctor is, "Here, take this medication, change your diet, exercise more, and I'll see you in three months." In our model, if that happens, the health coach is there before the visit to get to know the patient. The first fifteen minutes are just the patient and the health coach talking. Then the doctor comes in and joins what we consider the patient's team, and maybe brings in the behavioral health specialist or the nurse. The health coach has the last fifteen minutes of the visit, just one-on-one with the patient. A lot of this doesn't happen in traditional medicine. But what's interesting though is, if the doctor says, "Here, take this medication, exercise more, eat less and we'll see you in three months," the health coach's job is to say, "Do you have access to healthy foods? Do you have access to food? Can you stop smoking? What would prevent you from walking more? Do you live in a safe neighborhood?"

At the heart of the One Medical model is the demonstrated financial effectiveness of knowing the people it serves, and the improved outcomes that reduce the cost of care and more than covers the cost of having staff hear their patients' stories.

It has become commonplace to believe that scaled systems cannot be as focused on individuals, cannot rely on the relational approach that storytelling and active listening require. However, organizations like One Medical, Groups Recover Together, and SNHU are showing that human-centered work at scale is possible and sustainable when we take the time to really know the stories of those we serve.

Commencement ceremonies at SNHU always strike visitors as celebratory, warm, and unusually personal given the size of the crowd. Much of that is because of the profiles and stories of our graduates. Unlike most traditional graduations with mostly young people walking across the stage, our graduation ceremonies have incredible diversity: traditional-age graduates surely, but also veterans, parents (some holding babies as they come to the platform to receive their degrees), graduates in their sixties, seventies, and eighties—even one who was ninety-two, in a wheelchair, and with a guide dog—and those of many races and ethnicities, some wearing robes embellished with an aspect of their national dress.

As the university president, in full regalia that includes a large silver chain, university medallion, and a vaguely medieval hat, I act as master of ceremonies and tell the story of that day, of the graduates, and of the importance of their accomplishment. I often seek out individual and inspiring stories to share. One year I went off script and asked graduates to stand up if they were veterans or parents or first-generation Americans, the video of which became our best-known television commercial and the one that generates more interest from prospective students than anything we intentionally produced. Their stories are powerful.

Our fall 2021 ceremonies were particularly large, as we needed five ceremonies over three days to make up for the classes of 2020 and spring of 2021, which had their ceremonies postponed because of the pandemic. Thousands of graduates and their families traveled to the SNHU Arena in Manchester, New Hampshire, for the ceremonies (many stepping foot in the state for the first time), one on Friday and two each on Saturday and Sunday. In each one I stood for hours handing diplomas to graduates as they had their moment in front of the crowd. Families cheered loudly as their graduates crossed the stage, and one little girl could be heard above all the rest shouting, "Go Daddy, go Daddy, go Daddy!" as her father went up for his diploma. At the end of each ceremony, the graduates marched out of the arena, through a passageway and a large overhead door into a parking lot, where they had earlier assembled and would now disperse to find their awaiting families and friends. It has become our tradition for the scores of staff who volunteer to work the event to line up on each side of the passageway and clap the graduates out. It always surprises them a little, and many get teary as they bask in that last little bit of adulation.

I never participate in the clap line. By that point, my legs are weary, I have to pee, and I desperately need hand sanitizer. Graduates are often nervous when they come to the stage, and I shake a lot of sweaty palms. On this particular weekend, we had a pandemic still going on, and I was desperate for my bottle of Purell. However, for the fifth and final ceremony, I lingered at the very end of the line, just by the edge of the large overhead door, to watch the graduates leave. One noticed me, stopped, and asked to take a selfie. He then told me that, like me, he was the first in his family to graduate from college and how proud his deceased father would have been. By the time he finished, three other people were waiting in line to also take photos. I asked each of them about the day and how they came to us. One had started while still enlisted and deployed abroad. Another said she had started her studies twenty-four years earlier, then married and had kids, and was now finishing what she had started. One took both my hands in hers, shared that she had multiple operations in the previous twelve months, and with tears in her eyes (and mine), she said she wasn't always sure she would see this day. When I looked up, the line stretched through the door and far out into the parking lot.

Person after person stepped up, took a photo, and then paused to share a bit of their story. I held babies; met family members; hugged a man whose wife had been killed in a car accident just months before and whose photo adorned the mortar board on his head, a mother and daughter who graduated together, and a woman who gave birth and just four hours later hit the Send button on her last college assignment.

The line grew and some of the staff noticed that something special and unplanned was going on. A few rushed over to grab cameras and speed up the photo taking a bit, others hung a banner over the forklift behind me so the graduates would have a better picture, and some just listened, as I did, to these amazing stories. It had been a long weekend; I was exhausted, and yet I could not tear myself away.

This was the highlight of commencement weekend for me because stories have power. And while I had presided over the five ceremonies as storyteller-in-chief, I was now a collector of stories and had a sacred role that went back to our preliterate ancestors sitting around a fire telling stories. I was being asked to listen, to remember, to share, and to find in the collective stories a larger truth. In this case, the more collective and true story of SNHU: the triumph of our graduates, and the knowledge that what they worked so hard to accomplish mattered.

As a kid I had learned to tell stories. As an adult and a leader, I've learned to listen to them. Telling and listening is the double-edged tool that can ensure we keep people at the center of our work, recognizing their humanity and value while challenging ourselves to be ever better and not lose our way in a sea of data, efficiency reports, and technology.

THE PROBLEM OF SCALE

When I was president of tiny Marlboro College, with just over three hundred students at the time (smaller than a single lecture class at many large universities), donors always asked, "How is a place so small relevant in the broader landscape of higher education?" In terms of scale, the college wasn't remotely relevant. But in terms of efficacy, it was an extraordinary little place. Almost two-thirds of its graduates went on to graduate school, often to the most prestigious programs in the country, and outside examiners on senior projects routinely gushed over the quality of the students' capstone work.

Marlboro performed at that high level while unselective in its admissions, with limited resources, and no scale whatsoever. Its success was built around one core approach to learning: deep knowledge of each student, giving them agency in their learning, and providing relationship (with support and mutual accountability) in community. In many ways, it was a pure and ideal expression of learning—so much so that Loren Pope, the longtime higher education editor for the *New York Times*, considered it one of his two or three favorite colleges in America, and the MacArthur Foundation awarded it a grant for the genius of its model, a play on the "genius grants" to talented individuals for which the foundation is so well known.

I was incredibly proud of the education model but also incredibly frustrated that it did not at all speak to the enormous challenge of scale and the need to educate more people at lower cost. Those in the know admired it but in the way of a precious bauble or a curious artifact not quite of the world they inhabited. Indeed, it required so much philanthropic support to survive, became so expensive, and provided so few of the other attributes that attract students (location, amenities, size, connection to work, sports) that it finally closed in 2020. Yet the lesson it taught me, echoed in the most impactful learning I had growing up, was the centrality of human relationships in effective learning.

While I learned the language of mattering and intersubjectivity later on, I had experienced and seen firsthand at Marlboro the power of human relationships in learning and personal growth. It's hardly a revelation. We know that a fitness program always works better when we are going to the gym with someone else or working with a trainer. We all could read a textbook on any given subject, but we enroll in classes to be with other humans, teachers and students, when we genuinely want to learn something. How to scale the power of relationship— whether in education, health care, criminal justice, mental health, or any area where people want to learn, heal, and grow—is something that I have wrestled with ever since my time on that small, bucolic Vermont campus.

Do we need scale? The challenges of education, health care, mental health, substance abuse, and criminal justice exist at scale. That is, the needs are measured in tens and hundreds of millions. For example, twenty-eight million Americans do not have health care; 60 percent of Americans over the age of twenty-five have no college degree in an age when postsecondary education is increasingly critical to having meaningful, good-paying work; our country annually educates over fifty million students in its public schools (a single city, New York City, educates more than one million students in its K–12 public school system); over fifty million Americans, one in five, live with some form of mental health issue; and over two-and-a-half million children are homeless.[1]

The problems are staggeringly big, and while local solutions are usually effective and inspirational, they are often hard to render in systematic, sustainable, and thus scaled ways that might effectively address the issues.

The challenge also takes place in a distinctly American culture of individualism, unfettered capitalism, and an increasingly dysfunctional government that has limited commitment to the communal good, is punitive toward the disadvantaged, and is reluctant to ask the wealthy— whether individuals or corporations—to better support the citizenry through a more equitable distribution of income in the form of higher taxes. While the US absolutely has the wealth and resources to effectively address the human challenges of society, it refuses to do so.

But investing more is not wholly the answer. For example, the US spends more per person on health care than any other country on the planet, yet it has worse outcomes than many.[2] Our nation spends more per pupil on K–12 education than almost any other Organisation for Economic Co-operation and Development country, yet our students perform more poorly than most.[3] The massive healthcare and education systems have mixed outcomes at best, and routinely dehumanize the people they serve. To the extent that the people they serve are poor or non-White, systems and organizations are predictably more bureaucratic, yield even poorer outcomes, and are more dehumanizing than those that serve wealthier and White people.

I am driven to have SNHU serve as many people as possible. The need for high-quality, affordable postsecondary education is enormous in our society, with far too many people being left behind in an increasingly inequitable economy. Our students include the nearly forty million Americans who have some credits, student loan debt, and yet no degree—the worst kind of trifecta—and need to complete that degree they started in order to unblock economic opportunity for themselves.[4] Because of our large student population, we have built a scaled operation. But we have also tried to maintain a personalized, highly supportive focus on individual students, which is critical to supporting students in the challenging open-admissions sector in which we operate. Our students are more likely to fail because of financial reasons, life circumstances, scarcity of resources including time, or the internalized baggage that comes with poverty, race, and past struggles than for any intellectual or academic limitation.

For our academic model to work, and to realize our mission to transform lives at scale, we have to make our offerings affordable (we haven't raised tuition in over ten years) and use technology, data, and systems to scale up, all while keeping the individual student at the forefront. We need to make each student feel like they matter, support their aspirations, hear their stories, and serve them in a massively scaled system that still provides the highly personalized experience they need to succeed.

Our scale provides all sorts of advantages that include amortizing the cost of operations across a greater number of students (while our total dollars spent is quite large given our size, our spending per student is lower than many others), collecting enormous amounts of data that can be used to improve our efforts (we have more than seventy people working in data analytics alone), and reducing the cost to students for resources like textbooks.

Scale provides enormous advantages. For example, HCA Healthcare is the country's largest health-care company, with 183 hospitals and nearly two thousand care sites across twenty-one states and in the UK. By standardizing systems and leveraging its scale, HCA Healthcare can efficiently serve many more people than other health-care companies (one in every seventeen babies born in the US is born in an HCA facility[5] and its maternal mortality is less than half the national rate[6]), generating revenues of more than $50 billion, which funds more acquisitions and its organizational reach.[7] Scaled systems also generate so much more data than unscaled systems, providing greater insight in performance. HCA used data from over fifty thousand surgical procedures to put in place new protocols that reduced the length of hospital stays and cut the use of morphine-equivalent medications by half.

Before the pandemic, representatives from other universities visited SNHU almost every month. Before their visits, they often listed the subjects they wanted to explore, such as our technology, the design of our courses, our advising model, and our student recruitment strategies. However, the one subject they rarely listed—yet one that stopped them in their tracks during their visit—was the use of data.

We can monitor every online course 24/7, do predictive analytics, track student behavior, and drill down into individual assignments in any given course among the thousands we have running at any given time to flag places where students seem to stumble. The insights provided here support our student advising model and allow us to proactively reach out when we sense someone struggling.

The data analytics session usually runs late, as we get bombarded with questions. I remember one university president turning to his provost and asking, "Why can't we ask these kinds of questions and get these kinds of insights?" Scale and large numbers give us a growing and rich base of data from which to build insight.

There are great benefits that come with mere growth, but they can exponentially increase when we instead scale. I have sometimes struggled with the difference between *scale* and *growth*. Generally, scaling means being able to serve many more people with the same infrastructure and minimal additional investment. Growth means serving more people but adding commensurate expense. In the former, the gap between revenue and expense widens with scale, while simple growth usually sees revenue and expense track in lockstep.

In a for-profit world, the appeal of scale is obvious: greater and growing profit margins and higher stock prices for publicly traded companies. In a world of social services, say education or health care, scale allows more citizens to be served without greater demand for taxpayer dollars. For a private nonprofit organization like mine, scale provides greater surpluses, which in turn allow us to reinvest in the organization, take better care of our employees, and keep prices within the financial reach of students.

When it comes to the human-helping systems that are meant to improve people's lives and yet so often dehumanize them, such as many systems in education, health care, substance abuse treatment, criminal justice, and refugee aid, it's helpful to think of scaled organizations as a machine. To work smoothly, efficiently, and at scale, the machine wants repeatable and replicable processes, automated functions wherever possible, and highly defined components (whether systems, processes, or people). However, more scale often means less nuance and care for the human beings we serve.

In the previous chapter, I argued that leaders of people-centered organizations need to be collectors of stories, to hold multiple and myriad stories in hand, and that a willingness to surface conflicting narratives helps us understand what needs attention, the places where we can be better. Here's the problem: scaled systems do not like the messiness that comes with this story-collecting method of knowing. Scaled systems require taxonomies, categories, and rules-based processes.

Messiness, of any kind, gets in the way. Anything that doesn't fit the rational model, with all of its assumptions and necessary simplifications, is like grit in the gears of a large machine. As Anna Lowenhaupt Tsing argues in her brilliant book *The Mushroom at the End of the World: On the Possibility of Life in Capitalist Ruins*, "Arts of noticing are considered archaic because they are unable to 'scale up'."[8]

When we notice, listen, and collect stories, we are quickly reminded that we human beings are complicated, capable but self-sabotaging, graceful, mean, and wildly variable in our behaviors depending on the context in which we find ourselves. This is abundantly evident to any thinking person, yet we build systems that routinely ignore this reality. In other words, systems want to reduce our complex humanity to well-defined, if simplistic, categories and hierarchies that lend themselves to systems and scale.

Rachel Carson, CEO and cofounder of Guild Education, which works with employers and educational providers to educate and upskill workers, was inspired to create her company when she worked with community colleges and saw the power of coaching and the struggle to scale it:

We have tried to impose a nineteenth-century industrial model, which was designed to create products efficiently and at scale, on the work of helping people. In the industrial economy, we thought we could slice everything up and specialize people into parts, and that the system would bring all those component parts together. That works in a factory. That really doesn't work in education and health-care. So what did we do in health-care? We have a doctor for every body part. What did we do in education? We built a teacher for every subject. But we didn't have a person whose job—other than kind of internal care, which is the thing we pay the least and we value the least and we promote the least—[was] looking at the whole human. We did the same thing in education. We stripped out all the budgets of coaching, advising for younger grades, homeroom, whatever. We stopped investing resources in the whole person in education, the same way we did in health care. We thought we should just specialize it.

As Tsing notes, "scalability banishes meaningful diversity, that is, diversity that might change things."[9] In scalable systems, policies become inviolate, human judgment constrained, and the needs and workings of the system trump the needs of the individuals who the system seeks to serve.

Here is a simple and recent example: A prospective student emailed me to share her displeasure with our transfer credit policy. Like 80 percent of our online students, she had credits previously earned by taking classes at other schools, and she wanted as many of those as possible to count toward her desired program with us. However, our policy on accepting such credits requires them to have been earned within the last ten years. This student had received an A in college algebra eleven years ago and asked if the years really made such a difference and if algebra, invented in nineth-century Persia, had changed much since her enrollment. At my direction, we waived the policy and accepted the credits. But how many others were needlessly losing credits because the system decided and enforced a rule no matter the circumstances of the individual? My other worry is that perhaps our culture, working within a larger and more complex and rule-bound system, is impeding the ability (or willingness) of our people to do the right thing for students.

There are many more high-stakes examples of scalable systems that put system rules before human needs. Few are as onerous as mandatory minimum sentencing laws that remove judicial discretion and ignore context. Consider this testimony from Jay Rorty of the American Civil Liberty Union's Drug Law Reform project:

> I told the commission the story of an ACLU client, Hamedah Hasan, who received a life sentence for a first-time, nonviolent drug offense under the most extenuating circumstances: she came to stay with her cousin in order to flee a physically abusive relationship, and the cousin roped her into running errands for his drug conspiracy. Despite her previously clean record, her sentencing judge found his hands tied by a combination of mandatory minimums for crack cocaine and the then-mandatory sentencing guidelines based on those minimums. Hamedah's sentence has since been reduced from life to twenty-seven years, but she still has ten years left to go. Hamedah has three daughters and one granddaughter. She gave birth to her youngest child in prison, and because of the ripple effect of this sentencing structure, Hamedah's children and grandchildren are growing up without her.[10]

By contrast, many forms of Sharia, the Islamic legal system much misunderstood and maligned in the US, are built around contextualized judgment. You and I may commit the same crime, but our sanctions can differ quite a bit depending on our circumstances and the community's needs. When it works, sanctions respond to the individual human being and are adjusted accordingly. To many of us, that can sound unfair because we have an abstract notion of equal justice. But individual human circumstances are never equal.

Scale and the dehumanization it often includes can go horribly wrong, exacting a toll on those it impacts and becoming dangerous. For example, dehumanization is a prerequisite for violence, and systemic dehumanization can descend into widespread persecution, cultural obliteration, and even genocide. Tsing illustrates that notion with the example of the Klamath tribes in Oregon and California as logging interests sought access to their protected lands:

> In the 1950s, scalability was a matter for citizenship as well as resource use. America was the melting pot, where immigrants could be homogenized to face the future as productive citizens. Homogenization allowed progress: the advance of scalability in business and in civic life. This was the climate in which legislation was passed to unilaterally abrogate U.S. treaty obligations to selected Indian tribes. In the language of the day, members of these tribes were said to be ready to assimilate into American society without a special status; their difference would be erased by law.[11]

Michelle Alexander's 2010 book *The New Jim Crow* is a searing indictment of the American criminal justice system, a system grounded in the systemic and racist dehumanization of Black people, and its systematic and scaled assault on Black communities. The most heinous example of scaled dehumanization is the Nuremberg Race Laws of 1935, which laid the basis for the systematic exclusion of Jews from most aspects of public life, including civil service, universities, professions, and much of the economy. What followed was one of the darkest chapters of human history.

It may seem a dark turn to associate scalability with the assimilation and eventual obliteration of Native Americans, structural racism in criminal justice, or the Holocaust. But Tsing persuasively argues that the roots of commercial scalability that we take for granted lie in the use of enslaved people by Portuguese sugarcane plantations in the sixteenth and seventeenth centuries. It was a system that relied on transported people who were robbed of any relationships or community and thus isolated. She writes, "Already considered commodities, they were given jobs made interchangeable by the regularity and coordinated timing engineered into the cane."[12] Tsing cites Sidney Mintz's argument that the sugarcane plantations—with its model of interchangeable parts, including alienated workers who manned the machines—subsequently informed the industrial period.[13] Both the plantation system and industrialization reduced human beings to interchangeable parts without agency, authority, or differentiation to work at scale. Those principles have informed much of modern commerce.

Up until the 1980s, the excesses of Industrial Age capitalism were counterbalanced by strong institutions, including adequately funded public school systems, a federal government that could declare a war on poverty, federal courts to protect voting and civil rights, strong unions, and robust redistribution of wealth. (The marginal tax rate in the economic growth decades of the 1950s, '60s, and '70s was as high as 92 percent and never below 70 percent. Today it is 37 percent.[14]) Some of our best years in terms of economic growth coincided with years of our highest marginal tax rates,[15] and the idea that tax cuts for the wealthy fuel economic growth and are good for everyone, so called trickle-down economics, has been soundly refuted.[16] They instead lead to greater wealth inequality and less funding for the social systems meant to counteract the effects of poverty and lift people up.

In the human-helping sectors, those same principles of scaling in regard to workers and employees within systems have also been applied to the people who are being served. When we build scaled systems to serve categories of people, the volume of work usually leads us to segment our customers into groups with shared traits.

As SNHU grew, we struggled to think of and respond to the individual student in the same way we could when we were small and our fledgling systems were more malleable. It's true that the burgeoning fields of data analytics and machine learning are allowing for algorithmic attempts at personalization, but they are better suited to the analysis of consumer behavior and purchasing correlations like we see with Amazon and Netflix than to the messy and complicated work of bettering human lives. True personalization remains elusive in medicine and education, and algorithms have been shown to reflect the biases of their creators and overlook the complexity of human lives, such as the intersectionality that refuses to tell only one story of a person.

Take the case of a system built to handle, say, homelessness. If that system organizes itself to address the problem within that segmentation called homeless without the organizational capacity to also address other identities or segments such as mental health, substance abuse, and unemployment, its outcomes are likely to be poor. Likewise, so many universities have struggled and failed with their online programs because they treated students as a single segment and simply moved the programs created for traditional-age undergraduates online only to discover that the online student is a very different customer segment with needs that are different from their program offerings. While the traditional-age student living on campus wants a degree and a coming-of-age experience— joining clubs, playing sports, hanging out with peers, and generally discovering who they are—the thirty-nine-year-old married Iraq war veteran with two kids and a dead-end job has had all the coming-of-age he can handle. He wants a program designed to fit into his busy life, where family and job take precedence, at a price he can afford and that unlocks opportunity as quickly as possible. Schools that fail to make the distinction and understand the very different needs of these student segments invariably fail the ones who do not fit their system.

But note here that I still use the phrase *student segments*. We must build systems that better acknowledge and serve segments of students, but that level of segmentation cannot provide the individualized support that students need. For example, at SNHU we have dedicated teams (mostly made up of veterans or people in military families) for our military students because they want to work with staff who understand their experiences.

Our systems are well built for working adults instead of traditional-age students who want a campus experience. That's critically important to our success, but it isn't enough. It is our advising teams, which spend a lot of time with students and get to know them as individuals, that are most critical to our success because systems serve students but advisers are in relationships with them. It is because of interpersonal relationships that we can get an email such as this one:

> Let me start by saying that I appreciate that your recruitment staff and advisers took the time to visit with me and help me to realize the courage that I already possessed and urged me to take a chance on my future. When I received the call from Rachel S****, my adviser, I had reached rock bottom in my life and was unsure of how to continue forward. I had just moved back home from across the country after losing my job and becoming homeless only two years clean from a terrible five-year-long meth addiction and seeing nowhere to go but back into my addiction. Your school gave me the hope and strength that I needed to pull my life back together and strive toward a purpose that was greater than myself. Here I am now, only two terms from completing my degree with a 3.9 GPA and I now have the confidence and courage to look forward to applying to graduate school. I now have hope.

Customer segmentation can't do what Rachel, this student's adviser, did when the student was teetering on the brink of failure. Only a dedicated person in relationship with another person, letting them know they matter, helping them hope, and hearing their story can do this work. Not a system, a chatbot, or an algorithm.

Knowing Who We Serve

So much consumer data is collected about us that it is common to believe that "they" already know everything about us. This can be particularly true in terms of our consumer behaviors, with online retailers, credit card companies, and streaming media services tracking our searches and choices and purchases. However, for the complex work of education, health care, social welfare, and other human-helping sectors, the complexity of human beings defies the algorithms, which remain unable to code trauma, irrationality, hope, grit, fear, and the other mysteries that make people, well, people.

The reason we can serve students at scale while making them feel they matter is that each student has an academic adviser, like Rachel, who is more like a life coach accompanying them in their learning journey. While those academic advisers are there to help with course selection, prerequisites, access to tutoring, and so on, so much of their work is about understanding the student in a holistic and individualized way and supporting them in the particular ways they need.

One Medical's Alexander Packard describes a similar model in which health-care coaches are responsible for genuinely knowing the individual patient and helping them manage their health in ways that the system does not encourage.

It extends that model to its clinicians as well but retrains them in a way their medical education did not—namely, to understand the human being sitting on the examination table. Alexander says:

We do case reviews and chart reviews. Clinicians get together to review a particular case and say, "Well, how should we proceed here? What does the patient want? What are the patient's values? What does their family want?" That's a kind of training that we haven't found available in the outside world that we've had to build ourselves.

Colleen Nicewicz attributes Groups Recover Together's success rate in treating opioid addiction, which is two to three times higher than the industry average, to care navigators who understand that successfully treating addiction means understanding the full spectrum of a client's needs. She explains:

We like to plug into the community. We have people on our teams called care navigators, who are helping our members—we call our patients "members"—plug in with different parts of the community. They're coming to us for their treatment an hour a week for as long as we mutually agree upon. Outside of that, we're helping them get housing . . . food is something that they need. We're helping them re-engage in a healthy way with the health-care system. We're trying to get them to find a primary care physician or help them get to the dentist. We have teams of people [doing this work] When our members come to us, their distrust of the health-care system is at its highest. They rebuild that trust with us. Then they looked at us to say, "OK, well, I guess I am ready to go see a primary care doctor. Who should I go to?" They look to us to help them navigate the overall reentry into the health-care system.

In all of these models, the staff person closest to the client—whether a student, patient, or addict—is the critical actor because they know the whole person and build relationships. Colleen explains:

The logic is that the clinical person is the one who's spending the most time with the patient. The doctor's coming in once a month and saying, "Hey, how's your medication? Is it making you sick? Are you doing okay?" But there are four other hours that month that the person is struggling, talking about all the other psychosocial issues that they're managing. The idea is that the counselor is the point person who somebody can pick up the phone and call. The rationale is that they are receiving the highest volume of the patient connection. They're managing that relationship. When you read any of our reviews or patient testimonials, it's the counselor who they attribute their success to. It's not the doctor . . . It wasn't the person who prescribed them the medication, although they find them helpful, for sure. It's the person who helped me problem-solve how to get my kids back or helped me figure out how to get a job. That's where they're making the personal connection.

Emily McCann, the former CEO of Citizens Schools, argues that those who engaged with students every day were successful because of the relationship building and knowledge they had. And that, she says, fueled system improvements:

The majority of the innovation that was happening within our organization was led by the people who are closest to the work, whether those who are working directly with the communities implementing our system or those who were working with the teachers.

Research funded by the Gates Foundation made clear that one of the biggest impacts on student persistence is found in professionalizing and supporting student advising.[17] The deep connection and knowledge of who we serve not only works against dehumanization, but it also results in a system that produces better results, and that connection to those served helps produce a better system, a system that knows in very deep ways the people it seeks to lift up.

This approach is not simply for boutique organizations. Until its acquisition by One Medical, Iora had forty-seven facilities across eight states[18] and treated more than thirty-nine thousand patients per year.[19] Using a similar coaching model, SNHU serves more than one hundred eighty thousand learners. Citizen Schools is a national organization serving more than two hundred thousand students. The more patient-centric approach that Lorris Betz led was in a health-care system serving more than twenty-two thousand[20] patients per year. Scaled systems and organizations do not have to dehumanize the people they serve, but they have to care enough not to, and that requires genuine human relationships.

Why Mission Matters

Mission statements keep us honest. Or, at least, they can provide a reality check on what we say about ourselves and then what we actually do. A mission statement essentially answers the question of why the organization exists, and it usually reflects the core work at hand and some sense of aspiration. It is also usually broad enough to allow for a wide range of actual activity. Here are some examples of company mission statements taken from their websites:

- TED: "Spread ideas."[21]
- Tesla: "To accelerate the world's transition to sustainable energy."[22]
- Starbucks: "To inspire and nurture the human spirit—one person, one cup, and one neighborhood at a time."[23]

- New York Public Library: "To inspire lifelong learning, advance knowledge, and strengthen our communities."[24]
- Patagonia: "We're in business to save our home planet."[25]
- Los Angeles Unified School District: "Embracing our diversity to educate L.A.'s youth, ensure academic achievement and empower tomorrow's leaders."[26]
- Amazon: "To be Earth's most customer-centric company, Earth's best employer, and Earth's safest place to work."[27]
- University of Utah Health: "University of Utah Health serves the people of Utah and beyond by continually improving individual and community health and quality of life. This is achieved through excellence in patient care, education, and research; each is vital to our mission and each makes the others stronger."[28]
- Louisiana Department of Public Safety and Corrections: "We achieve our vision through safe, secure prison operations and community correctional programs, development and implementation of effective criminal justice policies for Louisiana, and the provision of rehabilitative opportunities for imprisoned people that supports their successful transition into the community."[29]

And here are some examples of university mission statements (that can't help but be a bit wordier):

- Yale University: "Yale is committed to improving the world today and for future generations through outstanding research and scholarship, education, preservation, and practice. Yale educates aspiring leaders worldwide who serve all sectors of society. We carry out this mission through the free exchange of ideas in an ethical, interdependent, and diverse community of faculty, staff, students, and alumni."[30]

- The University of Alabama: "The University of Alabama will advance the intellectual and social condition of the people of the state, the nation and the world through the creation, translation and dissemination of knowledge with an emphasis on quality programs in the areas of teaching, research and service."[31]

- Brigham Young University: "The mission of Brigham Young University—founded, supported, and guided by The Church of Jesus Christ of Latter-day Saints—is to assist individuals in their quest for perfection and eternal life."[32]

- Southern New Hampshire University: "Southern New Hampshire University transforms the lives of learners. Our success is defined by our learners' success. By relentlessly challenging the status quo and providing the best support in higher education, Southern New Hampshire University expands access to education by creating high-quality, affordable and innovative pathways to meet the unique needs of each and every learner."[33]

Because these mission statements are aspirational, it's easy to poke fun at the ways they fall short or inflate their importance. Come on, Starbucks: it's only coffee—though my body, if not my spirit, is admittedly nurtured by the first cup of the day. However, language is powerful and words matter, so mission statements frame the essential big picture and raison d'être for organizations. They serve as North Stars for the work done by the organization and are often invoked to motivate, to pressure test strategic goals, and to maintain integrity of effort.

Therein lies the real value of a mission statement—to keep us honest. The mission statement is not a plan of action, a budget, a quality of culture, a road map for sustenance or profitability, or a list of specific outcomes. Indeed, Richard Chaitt, a respected scholar of governance, argued in 1979 that college mission statements enjoy exaggerated importance and that "the mission will always be, in some sense, survival"— that institutions will make whatever pivots are necessary and rewrite their mission statements to fit the bill. He argues that distinctiveness, getting better at what we do, and actions are what matter.[34]

I agree but believe there is real value in the mission statement as a reminder that our planning and resource allocation, our actions and attempts at improvement, and our focus should align with what we say about ourselves in our mission statements.

When we see organizations lose their way, it is often because their reality and actions do not align with why they exist. For instance, the University of Alabama paying its football coach $10 million per year has nothing to do with the "creation, translation and dissemination of knowledge with an emphasis on quality programs in the areas of teaching, research and service." As Laura McKenna in a 2016 article in the *Atlantic* points out, there is little evidence that big-name coaches and successful athletic teams result in admitting higher-quality students or more funds for the academic mission of the school. Even in those programs that bring in massive advertising revenues, the funds usually stay within the athletic department.[35] However, alumni, fans, and even local politicians demand winning programs, and for big-time programs like the one at Alabama, the athletics programs and their coaches are nearly untouchable. As the land grant and flagship university for a state in which 26 percent of the population is Black, only 11.6 percent of the student population on the main campus is Black.[36] Perhaps $8 million of that $10 million salary could be better spent.

In a world upended, where opportunities and threats are coming at us faster than ever and the stakes are often existential, the mission statement can bring clarity when making choices. Not certainty, which should be suspect in a volatile, uncertain, complex, and ambiguous world, where we need to always be learning and adjusting in response to our rapidly changing world. Certainty on how to act based on how we have acted in the past can get us in trouble when the game has changed.

Holding on to a mission is not an argument for holding on to how we have done things in the past. Clarity of mission means that no matter how we act, adjust, and respond—all needing to be done with greater agility and speed than was required in a more stable and slower-changing world—we are still heading in the right direction. In my own organization, we have been looking at acquisitions, and exploring new opportunities, partnerships, and investments at a pace and volume that is unprecedented for us and unusual in our industry. The question that begins and ends each of those inquiries, often asked by a board member or member of the leadership team, is whether we are being consistent with our mission.

In 2021, when the US was evacuating Kabul amid panic and chaos, a group of Afghan students reached out to me to ask for help getting family members out of the country. The fact that they had merely sent their daughters to an all-girls school in Kabul and then to America had put their lives at risk, and many had also worked for American contractors or the military.

Our international team leaped into action, with support from our general counsel and others, and began round-the-clock efforts to award student acceptance letters and full scholarships, get documentation into the hands of family members, coordinate with our congressional delegation, pay for flights out of Afghanistan, and work a network of military contacts.

My role was minimal—simply to approve the budget requests. At one point, we had committed over $650,000, and I emailed my board saying the cost would likely climb to over $1 million. The board's response? "Is that enough?" Similarly, we spend millions on our efforts to educate refugees and displaced people in Africa, Lebanon, and Haiti. Mission matters.

The Role of Money

It is often said that "every system is perfectly designed to get the results it gets," a quote sometimes attributed to W. Edwards Deming and sometimes to Paul Batalden, both noted management gurus. We might rephrase that and say we get the results we pay for. That is a bracing observation that invites us to ask hard questions of ourselves.

California spends $13.6 billion per year on its correctional system, and only 4 percent of that goes to rehabilitative programming.[37] The system's mission reads: "To facilitate the successful reintegration of the individuals in our care back to their communities equipped with the tools to be drug-free, healthy, and employable members of society by providing education, treatment, rehabilitative, and restorative justice programs, all in a safe and humane environment."[38] However, 97 percent of its budget is spent on warehousing and punishment. Is it any wonder that the formerly incarcerated suffer an unemployment rate of 27 percent,[39] are ten times more likely to be homeless,[40] and that 47 percent of them will wind up back in prison within three years[41] at a cost of $39,000 per year?[42]

The system invests in punishing people, which it does well, and ensuring safe conditions, which it does poorly, while woefully underfunding reentry programs that might actually deliver on what it says it does in its mission statement. This failure is not caused by the inmates being intractable (though their challenges are formidable) but by the system not mapping its investments to its desired outcomes, or at least its stated outcomes. That is true for most of American criminal justice, not just California. These are choices.

Higher education, the system I know best, abounds in examples of system attributes that work against student success. Here are just a handful of examples:

- Our experience at SNHU is that academic advisers, life coaches in many ways, play perhaps the most critical role in student success. Serving the same population, our results in many communities are three to four times better than those of local community colleges. One of the differences is the ratio of students to advisers, which is usually under 300:1 at SNHU and as high as 1,600:1 at some community colleges. As we now serve even more challenging student profiles, we are investing in bringing our ratios down. For whatever reasons, many community college systems do not or cannot, and it impacts their results.

- In much of higher education, a faculty members' promotion and tenure depends much more on their scholarship and publishing record than on their work with students. Indeed, the reward system of higher education usually links status to less, not more, time with students. On many campuses the students most in need of more time from their faculty are more likely to be taught by inexperienced teaching assistants or to find themselves in very large lecture halls with little to no direct contact with the teacher at the front of the room.

- When a student transfers from one college to another, they request that the credits they earned in their former college be accepted. Most colleges leave the decision to individual faculty members with disincentives to accept those credits.

For example, the faculty member and their program may be funded based on course enrollments, so accepting transfer credits squanders an enrollment and thus funding. Students are routinely denied credit for prior courses when they transfer, which drives up the cost of their education, increases the time to graduation, and creates inequities. For example, community college graduates—often students of color and lower income—frequently lose many of the credits they had earned when they transfer to a four-year institution, according to a 2017 Government Accountability Office report.[43] The report found that when that transfer was from a public two-year community college to a four-year public institution, students lost an astonishing 43 percent of their credits. Public institutions more often rely on enrollment rates for funding, so the system produces the result for which it was designed.

- In my book *Students First: Equity, Access, and Opportunity in Higher Education*, I argue that an education system built on the foundation of time—namely the credit hour—in which learning is fixed in terms of schedules and where students need to be when, fundamentally disadvantages lower-income students for whom time is less abundant and less in their control.[44] The book argues for non-time-based approaches to education that better suit the lives of students for whom time is a precious and rare commodity. Those who have more money have more time, or at least more control of it.

The corrupting influence of money in skewing values and mission is dramatically illustrated by Louisiana State University building a $28 million operations building for football, while its library sits in abject disrepair.[45] Only 13 percent of LSU's student body is Black, while 33 percent of the state's population is Black and earns just 50 percent of average income for the state. Largely White donors fund a lavish facility for a largely White institution that makes millions on its football program while not paying the players, who are 84 percent Black.[46] One might argue that the plantation system lives on, and looking at where money is and isn't spent speaks volumes.

Most of the innovators I interviewed for this project, all trying to rehumanize the systems in which they work, describe system incentives and how money flows as crucial contributing factors to the dehumanization of the people the systems serve. Many of the systems designed to lift people have third-party payers, often the government. In health care, it is likely insurance companies or the government (through Medicare and Medicaid). In K–12 public education, it is state and local municipalities. In higher education, it is often state and federal financial aid programs and, increasingly, employers. Prisons are funded by county, state, and federal government depending on where they sit in the country's massive incarceration system. (The US imprisons a higher percentage of its citizens than other economically developed countries, accounting for 21 percent of the world's prisoners with only 4.4 percent of the world's population.[47]) Those funding sources have competing aims, wanting to get the best outcomes for the least investment, letting simple scale supersede quality, protecting against fraud and abuse, and are often confused in their demands, a reflection of the politics that inform public funding of any kind. Private interests, for-profit and nonprofit, permeate these systems and have their own interests, including financial well-being, growth, and shareholder value in the case of publicly traded for-profits.

In terms of the broader context within the US, President Ronald Reagan ushered in forty years of increased privatization, antipathy toward taxes, distrust of government, and cost shifting from government to individuals. Of the dramatic budget cuts in Reagan's first term, 70 percent were in programs aimed at the poor.[48] In Republican-controlled state and local governments, a neo-Calvinist ethos of personal responsibility and personal benefit has come to inform funding approaches to public good. For example, a *New York Times* article reporting on higher education funding woes in Pennsylvania reports: "In a nutshell, the burden for supporting the system shifted sharply—from the state to the student. In the 1980s, the state paid 75 percent of a student's load. Now the student pays nearly 75 percent."[49]

Not only does this approach to systems funding lead to growing inequities and inadequate resources to get the work done well, but it also often does harm to the people who work within these systems. As Sara Goldrick-Rab points out:

> The first thing that immediately popped into my mind is the phrase "hurt people hurt people." You're talking about sectors that have, with few exceptions, been historically under-resourced and are well known for extracting a lot from their people for as little money as possible. That is the brutal part of the nonprofits. They try not to pay attention to money to the point that when they do get a new project, they don't hire new people. They just add hours to existing people and they burn them out. That's exactly what higher education has been doing for ages. The vast majority of the dehumanizing that I'm seeing is coming from people who are in varying stages of burnout. It's not just the people; it's the system they work in. But the system is made up of people, and even with the kinds of things that you do to adapt for people, there's not enough time to think. The vast majority of people who are interacting with students, shaping students, have no time for reflection time, have very little time for professional development time, and are incredibly under-supported in general.

Sara goes further to argue that racial animus informed Reagan-era social policy, and that the dehumanization of people of color in particular was intentional. Citing Reagan's infamous depiction of welfare queens, she says: "The way you take money away from people is, you dehumanize them and make them seem completely undeserving."

Dehumanization, as just described, is less of an outcome and more of a design feature intended to reduce the use of services. It is not only a question of decreasing the financial investment in human-helping systems that renders them less effective for the people they serve, but it is also the ways we design access to those systems. Pamela Herd and Donald P. Moynihan's *Administrative Burden: Policymaking by Other Means* is a superb exploration of the way administrative processes are used to achieve political aims often meant to render less service to fewer people, especially low-income and people of color. They offer this example:

> As far back as the Nixon administration, welfare programs have not been designed to balance take-up by eligible claimants with mistaken payments to ineligible beneficiaries; instead, administrative procedures have been used to reduce the former in the name of the latter . . . Welfare is also a domain where the politics of race play out, with robust evidence that burdens fall disproportionately harder on Black, relative to White, beneficiaries.[50]

These processes not only serve to depress use by those deserving and eligible, but they exact a psychological toll. Herd and Moynihan cite the 27 percent of those eligible for food stamps who won't use them because of how they must be used, signaling to everyone else in the grocery line that one is poor and shaming the user of the benefit.[51] If one believes that the working poor are poor and in need of benefits because they are lazy and thus undeserving, one can then design the system to inhibit the actual use of the service that can help them. In the case of food stamps, electronic benefit cards remove the stigma of using the benefit and improve uptake, but only if that is what the design of the system desires.

Former US Secretary of Education Arne Duncan recalled his eight years heading the Chicago Public Schools system, the third largest school district in the United States. Simply focusing on completion rates of Free Application for Federal Student Aid (FAFSA)—the required form necessary for a student to receive federal financial aid for college—which were under 30 percent in a system in which 85 percent of the kids were below the poverty line—unlocked billions of dollars of aid for students.

In contrast, where there is no undeserving "other," say in the case of Social Security, which benefits all, we make the process easy and straightforward, and the program remains popular across political lines. Not because it was easy to implement, as Herd and Moynihan point out, but because the objective was clear and simple, and it was designed for everyone.[52] When we all benefit from a system, we want that system to be respectful and straightforward and adequately funded.

While Herd and Moynihan described policymaking through intentionally designed administrative burden, system hurdles can be more benign. When we set out to scale SNHU's online operation, I assembled the then-small team of staff working in that area and hauled out a portable whiteboard. Standing there, erasable marker in hand, I asked them to describe to me all the steps that would have to be completed by a student or by us to take the student from initial query to actual enrollment. While they described the many steps, decision trees, and pathways in the process, I charted everything out on the whiteboard. At the end of the exercise, the board looked like the electronics schematic of a nuclear submarine. It was a wonder anyone enrolled. And this was a process mostly of our own design! We set out to simplify and reduce the process, making it as seamless as possible for students.

Arne's FAFSA example speaks to the ways we make it hard for many to access money available to them, but he also has stories about the ways we misspend money. His best example of rethinking the system happened in a school located in the third most violent neighborhood in the city. The principal called and asked to hire social workers instead of the security officers that accounted for about $100 million of system funding each year. While it made him nervous given the level of violence in that area, Arne OK'd the switch. He describes the outcome:

> It's funny. You run a big system. You think you know it all. You don't know it all. Their violence went down so much. We had an audit function. They went out to audit the school, because they thought they were lying on the numbers . . . I learned about all this after the fact, of course, but there was a 78 percent drop in violence in that school because they came at it in a very different way.

That principal spent no more on that system design decision but had remarkable results. All of the principals worked for the same desired outcome—safe schools—and all were dealing with similar budget lines. But one principal's decision to invest in holistically addressing the needs of individual students with social workers produced a much safer school than those who invested in managing the behavioral consequences of leaving student needs unmet. One might argue that the failure to get it right at most of those other schools was simply a result of poor decision-making. I suggest it is also a reflection of any scaled system's compulsion to avoid the messiness of understanding and serving individual human beings, with all their confounding complexity and messiness. Scaled systems favor strict rules-based ways of operating. Violate the conduct code, no matter the reason or context, and the system will respond, in this case with a call to the police. If the system has different organizational units performing different discrete functions, as almost all scaled systems do, then it is even more likely to lose sight of the individual in a holistic sense and the broader outcomes of the work.

Counterintuitively, the more expert the people within those segments or silos, the more diligently they do their work, the greater rewards they then enjoy when successful (including getting paid), the greater the likelihood that the system loses sight of the people it serves. Remember my mother-in-law, Rosella, in her dying days when her amazingly capable specialists lost sight of the overall picture and the person in the hospital bed in front of them? Here's the problem as described by Alexander Packard:

> At the end of the day, care is about relationships, but we've turned it into a series of transactions. We turned it into a visit or a procedure or a surgery or a specialist conversation, and we've packaged it and routinized it and distributed it across a lot of different areas of expertise that different medical professionals have. The process of trying to seek higher expertise—and maybe even higher revenue and higher efficiency and higher productivity—means we've effectively created a terrible system where nobody's really accountable for health outcomes. Everybody gets paid for doing something. I see you; I get paid for it. I operate on you; I get paid for it. I cut something off your skin; I get paid for it. When you reimburse for volume, what do you get? You get more volume. But nobody was really thinking about what heals, what has an impact, and the right payment model to encourage those better outcomes.

In Rosella's case, it was Christine, a nurse far lower in the hospital hierarchy than the specialist physicians, who worked with the whole human being lying on the hospital bed and finally called the specialists and family members together to look at the big picture. While the physicians would not order needless procedures, they were focused only on the part of the medical challenge to which they were assigned, were not assigned to the patient as a whole, and were working in a system that sees revenues only from doing more, not from doing less. Colleen Nicewicz echoes Packard's sentiments in the area of opioid treatment, observing:

A lot of the reason that is the case is because the way that people make money is not designed with quality in mind. The options out there for people were focused around things that didn't necessarily make them better—like a lot of testing that wasn't actually helping people manage their addiction. It was actually making them feel dehumanized and not actually getting at the problems that ultimately led them to their addiction in the first place.

Innovative providers like One Medical and Groups Recover Together had to persuade the third-party payers (health insurance companies and Medicare) to pay more for services that yield better outcomes—generally, services with more focus on the individual person such as more counseling sessions—than the outcomes yielded by easier to codify and measure actions such as testing, prescriptions, and surgical treatments.

System redesign of the sort described that produces better outcomes means there are winners and losers in terms of the underlying financial model, what and who receives compensation, and where status and authority shift. At Groups Recover Together, the quarterbacking of client care shifted from the medical staff to the counselor. At that high school in Chicago, fewer security guards and police on overtime detail were needed, but more social workers were hired. Often, these trade-offs provide better outcomes with lower costs to the systems, but those being displaced suffer a loss of income as well as status. So they often dig in and fight change, arguing on the basis of safety or quality.

Legislative attempts to allow lower-level health practitioners, such as dental hygienists, nurse practitioners, and optometrists, provide a great range of services, especially to lower-income patients often without care, have been met with robust opposition from lobbying groups and professional organizations representing the higher-paid clinicians who see a potential loss of income and status should they relinquish their hold on what services they alone can provide.[53]

When profit-making organizations are central players in a scaled system, the underlying financial model gets more complex still. The owners of for-profit entities in social service sectors such as education, health care, or criminal justice expect healthy financial returns for their invested capital. They can accomplish that by serving more people and charging for more services, while decreasing expenses—the basic building block of running any profit-making business. There are compelling arguments for including for-profit players in any social service industry, as they can be better than many (maybe most) nonprofits at finding savings and efficiencies, employing better and new business practices, and innovating for competitive edge.

For example, while the for-profit University of Phoenix (UoP) is often reviled by many in higher education, we should remember that in its earliest years it proved itself much better than nonprofit universities at accommodating busy working adults seeking degrees. It did this by employing modern technology, aligning its degree programs with in-demand jobs, and providing good customer service, a phrase that is still largely forbidden in nonprofit higher education (perish the thought that students deserve good customer service). However, when UoP became a publicly traded company with investors to satisfy (and investors only invest with the expectation that the profitability of the company will increase, with a commensurate increase in the value of their investments), the pressure to maintain dizzying growth rates and improve profit margins led to worsening outcomes, poor behavior, increased regulatory scrutiny, and a near toxic brand. UoP became the poster child for high-profit, low-performing higher education, and it and other for-profit universities were similarly taking advantage of students. At its height, the for-profit sector enrolled 12 percent of all college students and accounted for 50 percent of all loan defaults.[54] Good outcomes were sacrificed for profits.

This is not an argument against for-profit entities and the role they might play in human-helping sectors like education or health care, but a question of how an organization's mission can be subverted by inordinate focus on shareholder return, especially on a quarterly basis. As Rachel Carson says,

The idea of shareholder primacy is a myth. There have been no court cases, there is no body of law, there is no principle that the shareholders are the primal entity that the corporation is intended to serve or, more importantly, that short-term profits are the required optimization focus of any corporation. Milton Freeman's writings, perpetuated by the *Wall Street Journal* and the *New York Times*, created the myth that the corporation exists to maximize short-term gains, which has shaped today's capital model, which is really oriented around short-term earnings and the quarterly earning cycle, which in turn shapes the way corporations run their businesses. The short-termism is a way bigger problem than capitalism in its own right. What I don't think gets enough time and attention is thinking about what are the tools for long-term capitalism. Might the problem not be capitalism, but actually just be short-termism?

Nonprofits often face a similar pressure but from a different source of capital: philanthropy. Emily McCann describes that challenge at Citizen Schools:

> We talked a lot about impact, but the incentive was really around scale, and the money we were getting was designed to support the replication of this work so that funders could report a larger and larger number of students served. As we would look at our balanced scorecard—we were so proud of that—it had all these different dimensions. But the only thing we would ever talk about in these funder meetings was the "student served" number. I remember once it was twenty-five students lower than our goal, but our impact numbers were off the chart. And the question was, "What happened?"

She cites the irrationality and impatience of the philanthropic industrial complex when it pulls funding from solutions that are actually working for the people being served but take longer to scale. She says, "Philanthropic markets are not rational. It's not like raising series A, B, and C funding. You need to be "profitable" or have a surplus at the end of each year to be considered healthy, which is not true as organizations in the for-profit world are scaling."

In contrast, in over eighteen years of leading a large, scaled nonprofit university serving the same basic student profile as our for-profit competitors, I have not once been asked by my board of trustees about our surplus target (what would be called a profit margin in a for-profit context). While my team and I are expected to be responsible managers and stewards of our resources, there remains a laser focus on our mission to transform lives at scale and to make investments where needed. That includes forgoing any tuition increase for over ten years now, leaving tens of millions of dollars in students' pockets and not in our margins.

We enjoy much better outcomes than the for-profit sector, with higher graduation rates, much higher student satisfaction, lower tuition costs than most, and as our annual appearance on the *Chronicle of Higher Education*'s Great Colleges to Work For list attests, excellent working conditions for our employees. We are not morally superior or smarter than our colleagues in the for-profit sector, but their system is designed to prioritize shareholder expectations for a profit and valuation outcome, while ours is designed to prioritize student success. They cannot wholly ignore student outcomes because they would go out of business (many have because their student outcomes were so poor), and we cannot ignore our annual need for a surplus because we, too, would go out of business. The difference is priority, how much is enough, and then building a system that delivers with the right outcomes. If maximizing profits is the primary responsibility of the system and the people who lead it, the people served in that system are often secondary.

I have friends in the for-profit sector who like to argue that the only real difference between our institutions is tax status. They are wrong. The real difference is I am held accountable to our mission before anything else, whereas they are held accountable to their responsibility to build shareholder wealth and enriching ownership. In my world I also have to make the underlying business model work (thus the old axiom, "No margin, no mission"), but I don't have to maximize it to please investors.

The rise of the private prison industry, worth billions of dollars, starkly illustrates the consequences of putting profit ahead of human beings in a social service context. Here is what a scathing 2018 report from the Sentencing Project shows:

- States with private prisons incarcerate at rates substantially higher than the overall national averages—47 percent compared to just 9 percent nationally.
- Assaults in private prisons are double the rate of publicly managed prisons, attributed to fewer staff, less training, and higher turnover rates.
- Private prison companies actively support public policies (and organizations and politicians) that promote mandatory minimum sentencing laws, three-strike policies, and truth in sentencing laws, all of which lead to higher incarceration rates and more business for for-profit prisons.[55]

While public prison systems are mostly terrible, failing our need for community safety and the rehabilitation and reentry of those imprisoned, the report concludes that "the introduction of profit incentives into the country's incarceration buildup crosses a troubling line that puts financial gain above the public interest of safety and rehabilitation, and with limited transparency."[56] Our public prisons are bad; our for-profit prisons are even worse.

While nonprofit organizations may not put profit ahead of the people they serve, other dynamics can cause them to be less effective than they might otherwise be and even to lose their way in terms of mission. While profit-making per se might not be the purpose of the organization, nonprofits want to survive and, better yet, thrive. As a result, and likely because business people dominate their boards of trustees, principles of for-profit management permeate the nonprofit sector, especially when it comes to the notion of value creation. The simple idea here is that efficiency and productivity produce value, which contributes to lower expenses and greater margins. Can my highly paid professors and doctors serve more students and patients? Can I harness technology to

reduce the cost of delivering services? Can I use fewer correctional officers in my prison or cut back on the use of training programs?

In my own organization, I grapple with our extensive use of part-
time faculty (often called adjuncts) in our online operation. I know these
roles for us are not structured like traditional faculty roles, demand
much less (there is no course development, preparation, committee
work, scholarly activity, or other institutional responsibilities), and are
less central to the student experience in our model, which relies more
heavily on advisers than on faculty members. By reimagining the faculty role in this way, we can keep freezing tuition year after year and
maintain good outcomes while making the margins that allow us to
survive and thrive. Yet I worry about the 25 percent of our adjunct faculty who tell us they want full-time jobs and how well cared for our
adjunct faculty feel in our system. We are now reexamining how we
use adjunct faculty, asking whether we still have the right faculty model
for how we deliver education and whether we are treating our adjunct
faculty with respect and dignity.

The point is that the pursuit of scale and efficiency in nonprofits
can shape budgets in ways that aren't about enriching shareholders
but doing just enough in various parts of the work—particularly since
resources are often constrained.

The Role of People

To build on the earlier discussion of mattering, just as organizations
want to survive and thrive, the individuals within them crave agency
and authority, have basic human needs, and want to be treated with the
dignity that comes with mattering. They want a paycheck (to survive)
and to grow in their work (to thrive). Generally, the more hierarchical
the organization, the less authority and agency and dignity is afforded

to those on the lower rungs of the organizational ladder. As noted NYU psychoanalyst Jessica Benjamin points out:

> If you have a bureaucratic system, a cookie-cutter system, it's very hard to, within that, to give people the recognition they need—although some cookie-cutters are better than others. Work in general is not respected in our society unless it makes a profit for someone; the one who does the work is not respected. That's No. 1. But No. 2, service work is particularly not respected. A doctor can circumvent that to some degree by assuming the role of authority. So now I am the one on whom you depend, and I have the thing that you need. I am the authority who knows, and you are the one who does not know, who does not have what you need, who is dependent. You are the supplicant.

She describes the resentment of the powerless that can be acted out on the very people the organization or system is meant to serve. Anyone who has navigated a government bureaucracy in which a compassionless public employee has simply invoked a rule and flatly refused to consider one's circumstances has felt the receiving end of that resentment.

Alexander Packard describes the way he has tried to counteract hierarchy within the health-care system he leads:

> There were a bunch of things we did—no doctors' parking, no doctors' offices. Doctors sit with everybody else. We called doctors by their first name. No white coats. Even the staff would feel like, "Oh, the doctor is my colleague, not some hero I'm supposed to revere." We tried to equalize. Everybody sits around the huddle room table. At 8:15 local time at all forty-seven of our practices around the country, teams do the same thing: they do a huddle. Each day, a different person runs the huddle. It's not the person who's highest

THE PROBLEM OF SCALE

paid or has the most degrees. One day, the receptionist will run the huddle. The next day, the health coach runs the huddle. The next day, it's the behavioral health specialist. The next day, it's the doctor . . . It helps build team skills by bringing the group together, running a meeting, that kind of thing. Oftentimes, the doctors aren't that good at it. Health coaches really shine at getting the group together, running the daily meeting. It has a format. It has an agenda. That's empowering.

Similarly at SNHU, we have been trying to undo some of the hierarchy and bureaucracy that has set in with our scale, experimenting with communities of practice, employee resource groups, and empowering our student-facing employees to do the right thing for individual students without asking for permission.

We had a student in Ohio who was near completion in her degree but was going back into the hospital for yet another surgery, and the prognosis was not good. Her adviser and one of our IT staff, who was working to make sure she could stay connected while hospitalized, took it upon themselves to work with our registrar to capture her prior learning credits (sending her across the finish line), getting her diploma and having it framed, and then flying to Ohio on their own dime to present it to her. I still tear up when I think of the photo of them on each side of her hospital bed while she holds on to her diploma, beaming despite the tubes and monitors and fear of what might come next. We made sure to reimburse our staff and to shine a light on what they had done without asking for permission.

Lisa Dodson, in her book *The Moral Underground: How Ordinary Americans Subvert an Unfair Economy*, describes the way staff in organizations and systems routinely break the rules at risk to themselves to help people being poorly served by those organizations and systems in

153

which they work.[57] We want to build an organization that rewards, not punishes, doing the right thing. We have always taken good care of our people in terms of material benefits, providing award-winning benefits, healthy annual salary increases, low co-pays on top-level healthcare plans, and generous pension contributions. We are really focused now on that sense of authority, agency, and feeling of mattering that we believe translates into better care for our students. We want our people to choose connection with our students. As Jessica Benjamin describes it, they can't do that if they are "feeling depleted and deprived of recognition themselves."

Hamel and Zanini's *Humanocracy* shows how empowering employees at every level demonstrably improves organizational performance and offers a checklist of actions:

- Make the mission statement emotionally resonate for every employee.
- Help employees become less reliant on their managers.
- Expand their decision-making prerogatives based on their suggestions of where greater autonomy would help them better serve people.
- Institute team goals and rewards.
- Reduce distinctions of rank and hierarchy[58] (such as Alexander Packard did when he was president of Iora Health).

They describe this as community building, not organization building.[59] While Hamel and Zanini focus on for-profit companies, the challenge is no less formidable in nonprofits. For example, a 2021 internal poll conducted by Gallup for the Boston Public Schools system revealed that 52 percent of school administrators and central office staff are unengaged in their work, while another 20 percent were "actively disengaged"[60]— what Jessica would call being "busy acting out their unhappiness." We cannot build organizations and systems centered on the human beings they serve if we do not also build organizations and systems that respect and empower the people who work within them. If that is a test of efficacy, there is little evidence that the nonprofit sector is performing much better than the for-profit sector.

Finally, nonprofits can lose their way because the people they serve often have little other choice. If it feels like they do not care much, sometimes it is because they do not have to. Examples abound. Here are a few:

- Large public school systems serving families that do not have the means to afford alternative school options for their children
- State social service agencies that are the sole source of critically needed benefits for low-income citizens
- Jails and prisons, which have inmates who obviously have no choice but to be there and few advocates to address the routine dehumanization that happens inside

In almost every instance, these systems and the organizations within them are underfunded and lack the resources to honor their mission or provide good, high-quality service to the people they serve. Scarcity of resources, which makes everyone within an organization feel vulnerable, often leads to self-interest and self-protection, a kind of psychological survival impulse as principal motivator, instead of the good of those being served or the mission of the organization. The result ranges from benign neglect to poor services to outright hostility.

The combination of underfunding, misplaced investments and incentives, burnout and self-survival, limited competition, intentional administrative bureaucracy, and system limitations around scaling makes systems deaf to the individual human stories and needs of the people they are supposed to serve. In such systems, people feel they do not matter, their hopes are not supported, and their stories remain unheeded. These are systems that systematically dehumanize. Because the people these systems serve are captive to the systems, which face no real competition, those served have little ability to demand better and those working in the system are ill equipped to deliver better if they want to.

Building Human-Focused Systems at Scale

There is no one right way to get scaled systems and organizations to better serve and lift up those they are intended to serve given the range of needs, industry sectors, and organizations that exist in our complex society. However, there is a set of questions that might be asked of the leaders, policy makers, and reformers of any organization or system meant to help people survive, thrive, and flourish:

- Does the organization have a clearly defined mission?
- If it does, what does success look like? How would we know? What would we measure?
- Do its budget and its incentive and reward structures align with those measures of success?
- How well does the organization or system understand the people it serves? What are the ways it collects their stories and uses them to improve the work? How well does it understand and accommodate the individual person?
- Is the experience of navigating or accessing the services of the organization respectful and dignified? Does it communicate care?
- When those being served are asked to complete administrative processes, do those processes genuinely assist those completing them, or do they serve the needs of the system?

- Does technology replace human relations or amplify them?
- How does the organization hold itself and its people (starting with leadership) accountable?
- Do the employees closest to the work, who best know those being served, have agency and authority to act? Are they empowered? Is their knowledge and expertise fed back into the system writ large?
- To what extent does the organization work against traditional hierarchy in terms of decision-making, employee empowerment, and administrative bloat not directly tied to the services?
- Do the employees have the appropriate time, support, compensation, and working conditions to do good work for those served?

The best arbiters of performance are those being served. The questions we might ask them are:

- Do you feel like you matter to this organization?
- Do we give you hope and help you aspire to a better future?
- Do we understand and respond to your needs as an individual?

While we want an overall sense of the experience of our organization, we also need to ask those questions of each major area within the experience cycle because parts of the organization may excel, while others perform more poorly.

Fundamentally, getting the work right relies on making time and space for human relationships. When Lorris Betz recounts the dramatic turnaround he led in the University of Utah Health system, he described task forces, getting incentives right, and all kinds of system fixes, but when pressed, he focused on basic human relationships as being at the core of what was needed. He said patients want respect, communication, and understanding.

That same focus on connection and understanding is what One Medical's Alexander Packard described during his time leading Iora Health, what Colleen Nicewicz described at Groups Recover Together, how Ken Oliver described the reentry programs at CROP, what Emily McCann described at Citizen Schools, what Dennis Littky described at the Met School and College Unbound, and what is at the heart of our work at SNHU. It is not a nice-to-have add-on, a complement to the real work that needs to be done. In all of these cases, the relationship is actually the core of the work and everything else supports or complements it. It is a radical reversal that argues that successful scaling begins with making more, not less, time for human relations at a time when scaling strategies focus on reducing human interaction, employing more self-help, and deploying technology.

Scaling human relations, putting those served at the heart of the work, means understanding which interactions are merely transactional versus impactful. While we want every human interaction to be positive, the transactional tends to be task focused and the need is for speed, correctness, and ease. When a student wants to find out what they still owe for next fall's tuition, that is merely transactional and ideally managed by our technology and systems. When that student is worried that they might have to drop out, wonders if the extra sacrifices they are making to be enrolled are worth it, and wavering in their resolve, a warm, meaningful human interaction is needed. It's not always easy to know when the transactional is masking a more important impactful question or need, when "What is my balance?" is actually "Oh my God, how will I pay for college, and is this really something I should do?" This is where data and predictive analytics can amplify human relations, raising red flags and prompting proactive outreach before someone is in crisis mode.

In our case, if the system recognizes that a student has not spent much time logged into classes, has been absent from discussion forums, and has grades that are lower than we would expect, it flags an adviser who then reaches out. In health care, remote monitoring such as with sensors can support health coaches, who have actual relationships with patients. Scaled systems need to be smart about when someone needs a human.

Then the question is, Which human? Alexander Packard argues that there is too much social distance between most patients and most physicians. As he says:

> Our health coach role is based on a few philosophical points. One is that there's too much social distance between a patient and their physician. Even if it's not class difference—it often is class differ-ence, actually—most Americans don't know a doctor and aren't related to a doctor. There are only 750,000 doctors in the US out of a population of 330 million, so most people don't actually spend time with a doctor. Doctors are revered in our society. They wear white coats. They get special parking. They have offices and fancy degrees. We don't call them by their first name. We felt like that sheer social distance was really hard to bridge.

So during Alexander's time as president, Iora made health coaches the linchpin of its patient relationship, getting the right person for the role. Similarly, there is evidence that in college, first-generation students and students of color, who are often struggling with impostor syndrome and self-confidence, are more reluctant than their peers to ask a fac-ulty member for help, fearing that doing so signals they are not smart enough or don't belong. Similarly, in a grant-funded project at SNHU, we placed older students in the class as peer tutors. Struggling students reluctant to approach their professors readily approached the tutors, especially if the tutors looked like them, and we saw persistence rates and grades improve in those classes.

An important point here is that with both health coaches and tutors, increasing human interaction didn't mean taking more time from the most highly paid, highly trained people within the system, physicians and professors, which would have made the proposition much more expensive. It even showed that physicians and professors would be the wrong people to engage in those situations. That is not an argument for displacing highly trained and highly paid people to replace them with lower cost labor. It is an argument for letting highly paid people do what they do best and recognizing that the critical human interactions that are needed for success may come from others who are better at that work. They all should work in harmony.

Jessica Benjamin's work around thirdness is important here. As she writes, "the third or thirdness characterizes the position that transcends the complementarity of doer and done-to."[61] When we get human-centered systems right, the student, the patient, and the prisoner move from a position of done-to to a position of thirdness with the teacher or adviser, physician or health-care coach, and prison staffer or guard.[62] In those relationships, they recognize each other's humanity beyond the roles they have been assigned to play; they collect each other's stories in ways that complete the picture of each other. Both are then impacted, both matter, and both are lifted up. The best teachers will tell you they learn from their students. The best physicians learn from their patients. The best leaders learn from their frontline people. As Yale's Matt Steinfeld explains, that state of thirdness allows the cared for and the caregiver to genuinely see each other:

My experience working in prisons and forensic hospitals is that guards view prisoners in a dehumanized sort of way, that they are different, and this is dehumanizing. When the guard sees the prisoner as more of a human—the recognition that "Oh, we're all people here"—and they see each other as living, breathing, and capable of creative generativity, they transcend their roles and both are better for it.

In our work with refugees, we have discovered that when we offer the same educational programs to the camp staff that we offer to the refugees they oversee, the relationship between them alters. They now share a third space as learners together. One of the most frequent things we hear from our employees is, "I don't want supervision, I want coaching." They are saying they want to be learners—"Don't tell me what to do, teach me how to do it and be in it with me." The best coaches know success is not rooted in games, when they are on the sidelines, but in practice, when they are in the middle of the floor or field with their players.

Every time someone signals to us their need, we have to make sure the conditions and culture exist for our people to respond and to enter that third space with the person being served. That's the key moment of choice that goes back to our three framing questions of mattering, investing, and responding. As Jessica says:

If one nurse who's running the station is looking every way but at you when you're waiting to talk to them, and is dismissive and is conspicuously talking on their phone or something else, and another one is chatting with you and asking how your relative is and making a connection with you, the second nurse is saying, "I choose connection." This is very important, because every time you choose to recognize another person, you're choosing connection. Every time that you become the recognizer—not just the recognized—you are choosing connection.

As she explains, it is in that connection that we empower and restore dignity to people: "the underlying principle of recognition of others' humanity and recognition of their agency and their authorship, their right to be agents, their right to have authority over themselves, to have their intentions, to have a mode of expression, those basic things."

The magic here is that when we do that for the people we serve, we also benefit. The system gets better, smarter, more humane. When we use the phrase *scaled system* or *scaled organization*, we almost always associate it with poorer experiences, unsatisfying one-size-fits-all quality, and the dehumanization that prompted the exploration I've undertaken in this book. There may be a way to make scale humane.

New Systems Thinking

When we build our systems and organizations around the concept of relationship, we inevitably confront macro-level constraints and demands that work against a human-centered approach to the work. For systems that receive public funding, it can be people's unwillingness to pay more taxes and adequately fund the work, or ideological resistance to helping those in need, or racism and classicism, or mere indifference. For private or for-profit systems and organizations, it can be the pressure to increase profit or shareholder value. For regulated systems it can be forms of stakeholder self-interest (think of dentists fighting to restrict what dental hygienists can do), fear of fraud, and antiquated rules.

There are imaginative, innovative leaders reframing the work, finding new models, and working on scaled solutions that are genuinely human centered. Rachel Carson of Guild Education says, "I don't think there has to be a conflict between human-centered design and scale." She argues that technology and systems are important to manage repetitive tasks at scale, while we need to emphasize people for the thinking and feeling tasks:

> Our view at Guild is that technology increasingly and mistakenly serves specialized-use cases. Our coaches get asked the same question, across hundreds of coaches, probably five thousand times a day. That's a great question to have a chatbot answer. But then there's that student who today is going to ask a question that is specifically tied to their context, their lived situation, their human experience. They want a coach to answer that question. We talk a lot about how you make sure that you are using technology to scale the repetitive and using the meaningful human resources to focus on the cognitive, and just the difference between which tasks are repetitive and which tasks are cognitive. Because we for so long lived with systems training us all to be factory workers, we had humans trying to get really good at things that are ultimately repetitive. Now we're in the knowledge economy; we're in this seismic switch of trying to help people figure out how to focus on cognitive and human relational tasks, because the technology's going to do all of the repetitive tasks.

Rachel knows when profits are the primary goal. Especially in the short term, there is inordinate pressure to minimize the human in order to maximize profits. She is a harsh critic of what she calls short-termism, the expectation of growing shareholder return on a three-month cadence. She says:

> That's really important when you're talking about human scale, because often when you've got a human-centered design, you have a lot of human-centered costs, and all of those can be driven towards efficiencies over time, but it takes way longer. Which is why

if you interview any venture capitalists, they're like, "Ugh, health-care and education and these complex systems take so much more patience and take patient capital. We're just not really a system designed for that right now." If it were strictly the function of GDP, you would see way more get invested in those two sectors, and you don't because they don't scale on the classic economies-of-scale charts. They don't scale as fast as a whole bunch of other products. That's because it takes a lot longer to work out the kinks and figure out where you can create efficiencies in those models.

Rachel recently converted Guild from a traditional C corporation to a relatively new legal entity called a public benefit corporation (PBC), which now is allowed in thirty-five states. As she explains, "the most important thing is that when you are a PBC, you add your social mission to your legal charter and your board is obligated to uphold that mission." She sees the PBC designation as a buffer against short-termism and what she calls the myth of shareholder primacy.

As corporate law attorney Joshua Hayes explains:

The mission statement has real ramifications on how a PBC is run. With respect to a Delaware PBC's Board of Directors, the DGCL expands the factors that the Board should consider when making decisions. Unlike standard corporations, where the Board generally must consider maximizing shareholder value as its prime directive, members of the Board of a PBC must also consider both the best interests of those materially affected by the company's conduct, and the specific public benefit outlined in the company's charter. This can make decisions for directors of a PBC more challenging than those of a standard corporation, since these considerations can (and often do) come into conflict. This is why the DGCL also limits director liability by shielding directors from liability to the PBC's stockholders if they make a decision based on adherence to their mission as opposed to only considering stockholder profitability. So long as a PBC's directors' decisions are informed, disinterested and "not such that no person of ordinary, sound judgment would approve," such decisions are in accordance with the directors' statutory duties.[63]

While the 2019 decision of the Business Roundtable to push back on shareholder primacy and assert the responsibility of corporations to benefit all stakeholders—including customers, employees, communities, suppliers, and shareholders—garnered a lot of media attention, it was more a statement of intent.[64] Public benefit corporations legally codify and demand such action, and companies such as Patagonia, Ben & Jerry's, Kickstarter, and Guild Education have embraced the challenge.

Another powerful and largely misunderstood and underappreciated legal entity for scaled and more human-centered systems is the co-op. For many Americans, co-ops conjure up an image of the local hippie-run food co-op, but modern co-ops cover a broad range of industry sectors, including manufacturing, health care, childcare, and myriad services. Howard Brodsky is a world-renowned expert on co-ops and the co-CEO of CCA Global, a company that manages a wide variety of co-ops with revenues of over $12.5 billion. As he points out:

> Worldwide, there are one billion members of co-ops, and actually 12 percent of the world's population in some way is either working for or their work is directly related to a cooperative, some 250 million people. It's a significant part of our economy. There are co-ops that are $30, $40, $50, $60 billion cooperatives operating at massive scale.

Howard describes the contemporary cooperative as a platform for its members not only to find all they need to successfully run their business, but also to do much better financially. He explains:

A lot of the cooperative model is evolving to what we call platform cooperatives. Why does this matter? So much of our technology today is owned by large public companies in what I call the extraction economy, where a few people disproportionately extract profit in relationship to the workers who are doing the work. Let's take a technology like Uber that is driving massive inequality. What's happening is Uber's taking the biggest cut of the driver profit. These companies provide very little—in Uber's case, very little, except for the technology to align the customer and the driver. The company is not actually doing most of the work in the system. As a result, even though Uber drivers work long hours, after factoring in Uber's commissions and fees, their vehicle expenses and insurance, most Uber drivers don't earn much more than minimum wage. They're making very little. Contrast this to a new platform cooperative in New York City called The Drivers Cooperative, where the drivers own both the company and the technology, so on the exact same rides they were doing for Uber, drivers are earning 20 to 30 percent more in take-home pay. And drivers have board seat representation and get a real voice in setting company policy. Over five thousand drivers have signed up with the cooperative since launching in May 2021.

The Drivers Cooperative increases driver salaries by 30 percent while taking only 15 percent of each ride fare, compared to the 25 to 40 percent other ride-hailing apps demand. Globally, cooperatives routinely outperform conventional corporations, operating with better outcomes and lower operating costs while sharing the wealth more equitably among those they serve and those who work within them.

At SNHU we have drawn from the best practices of for-profit higher education such as using data analytics and integrated technology, offering good customer service, setting goals and holding ourselves accountable, and using standardized curriculum that is better aligned with workforce needs. We have also assiduously avoided the behaviors and practices that got so many for-profits into trouble and discredited the whole sector such as predatory enrollment tactics, high prices, low-quality programs, and regulatory corner cutting.

As a nonprofit, we suffer no pressure to satisfy shareholders or investors and no executive or board member gets a lucrative exit, so we can plan for the long term. On the other hand, we do not do many of the things that "real universities" do (that phrase is often used as a criticism of us) like research, big-time sports, trophy buildings, selective admissions, rankings seeking, reliance on philanthropy, or granting tenure to our faculty (though they have long-term rolling contracts).

In creating a kind of new hybrid model single-mindedly focused on students, we get skepticism from traditionalists who think we have become too much like the for-profits, and doubt from innovators who think we are still too much like a slow-moving nonprofit. Because we are regulated, we are frequently thwarted from doing what is best for students, whether launching and scaling new innovative programs that work better for students or wrestling with out-of-date regulations that could not anticipate the world in which we operate or the way we'd like to serve students.

Rethinking the model has allowed us to scale while giving students individualized attention and the better outcomes that come when you actually know and respect those you serve. Our overall Net Promoter

Score of 75.9 is exceedingly good, and the highest-rated part of the student experience is our academic advising with an NPS of 86, which is in Holy Grail territory (30 to 70 is considered great, and 70 to 100 is excellent. Apple has an NPS of 47, Amazon's is 62, and Netflix is 68).

When our students don't succeed, financial distress is the most often cited reason and is reflected in data from our student assistance service, Help University, which sees 40 percent of its inbound calls related to finances (the second most is related to reviewing benefits at 16 percent and health at 9 percent). It's almost never because of a lack of personalized care.

And a More Radical Proposal

With the Great Resignation prompted by the pandemic, we have millions of jobs going unfilled. However, I am in the camp who believes the current talent crisis will speed up automation and machine learning, with eventual displacement of jobs and lack of work for millions of people.

A 2013 research report from Oxford University predicted that 47 percent of jobs in the US are at risk of being computerized,[65] while a 2021 McKinsey Report projected that 25 percent of Americans will lose their job to automation, a more modest percentage that still means forty-five million out-of-work people.[66] Driverless trucks are taking longer to perfect than early enthusiastic projections posited, and the crisis in trucking will only impel more development and faster deployment.

As a presidential candidate, Trump railed against free trade agreements, but for every job lost to NAFTA, the US lost five to eight jobs to automation,[67] and we have only begun to see the impact as the development of artificial intelligence, automation, and robotics are advancing at exponential rates.

Consider the aforementioned driverless vehicles. A domino effect of consequences lies ahead that is about much more than transportation. We may need 100,000 more truck drivers today, but within ten years, autonomous vehicles will put some 3.5 million truck drivers—the number one middle-class job in twenty-nine states—out of work, along with another 3.4 million taxi, bus, ride-share, and train drivers. And with driving infinitely safer, expect disruption to the auto insurance industry. Indeed, the insurance and financial services industries stand to lose 7.2 million jobs because much of their work can be done by machines.

In response, there is growing interest in the idea of universal basic income (UBI), say $10,000 per year for every person. Experiments in the Netherlands, Finland, and Canada have been designed to make sure certain people are not penalized for working part-time (as they are in current welfare models) and are provided a basic safety net offsetting job displacement. But UBI has many challenges, including political— it's not clear free money is a winner for any political party—and practical. UBI's deeply regressive nature without means testing, the danger of a dependency mindset, and a poor cost to productivity ratio are all legitimate concerns. Worse, people derive enormous satisfaction and meaning from work, and UBI does nothing to address those deeply human needs.

Jamie Merisotis is president of the Lumina Foundation, and he and I have worked on a radical proposal for rethinking the work that people will do in an age of automation and massive job displacement. We have a huge need for more human workers across our societal landscape doing jobs that require compassion, creativity, and empathy—jobs that automation and robots will never do. The kind of human relations and connection in third spaces that I have been describing can never be automated. Imagine if we could flood our schools with more teachers and aides, and our mental health system and our nursing homes with more support professionals. What if music and art teachers were available everywhere?

We can put people to work in intensely human jobs, ones we do not currently fund or staff appropriately, through a human work initiative (HWI) that pays everyone a basic livable wage for work that can't be displaced, will make our society far better than it is today, and will provide enormous satisfaction to those who do it. With HWI, a working couple would have the means to buy a home, take a vacation, and have some savings. Moreover, they would live in communities with good schools, access to an array of creative pursuits, and would never worry about lack of care for an elderly parent or family member with mental health issues. There could be a range of HWI salary structures—maybe with people who have not developed their talent through formal learning programs at the low end, and people with jobs that require advanced skills and competencies at the high end. But no one able to work gets a benefit without working.

HWI would allow us to flood under-resourced fields with talent and fundamentally rethink whole areas of our society: free college becomes much more tenable, every city street would be safe because HWI would add public safety officers to our most needy communities, and so on. We would stop asking police officers to also be social workers, drug counselors, and mental health workers because those experts would be readily available when needed. For those who desire and can land higher paying jobs, say in creative jobs that robots can't do or ones that require ethical or moral judgment or the jobs that don't exist yet, HWI doesn't apply. In other words, HWI doesn't impede ambition or creativity. The enormous societal benefits of an HWI would extend to the economy, where increased purchasing power would drive consumer spending, construction, and other uses of discretionary spending.

The first and obvious criticism is the massive cost. Yet there are ways to make HWI affordable, including:

- A tax on robots, as Bill Gates has suggested.[68]
- Restructuring corporate tax around a profitability to human–employee ratio. Simply, the more people a company employs in relation to its financial performance, the lower tax it pays. Conversely, a company that enjoys enormous financial reward by replacing its employees with robots would pay more in taxes.
- Calculating the enormous financial savings of reductions in incarceration and crime in general, as well as financial gains from improved public health and the well-established gains from having a more educated citizenry.
- Rechanneling current expenditures for welfare and other related entitlement programs. Much of the $390 billion we spend on safety net programs could be redirected because they offset the impacts of unemployment and low income.

Rather than massively expanding the pool of public employees, HWI funds could be funneled through co-ops, newly created B corporations (which legally do not need to maximize shareholder value as their primary goal), and conventional companies so as to ensure the efficiencies and accountability of the private sector. If technology is radically remaking our world, we need to radically rethink our system of organizing and paying for the human work we so desperately need and that can create the foundation of scaled human work with relationships at its center.

We live in a broken world, and to the extent that unfettered capitalism, technology fetishism, and the gap between haves and have-nots (defined not only by wealth, but by race and gender as well) is structurally reinforced, we will not fix it through policy debates, regulation, more technology, or nostalgic calls for a lost world that was never really paradise and has failed too many of us in too many ways. As psychologist Steven Botticelli observes:

> If it was already the case, as Tocqueville observed of 1830's America, that democracy seemed unconducive to the maintenance of strong attachments between people (Bellah et al., 1985), the conditions of contemporary capitalism have only rendered this more true (e.g., Sennett, 1998).[69]

Ours is an age of fleeting commitments. Employers no longer have the long-term sustained commitment to their employees, and their employees, in turn, rightly feel little loyalty. This gig labor, now done by some 13 percent of all Americans and much more so by people of color, means short-term and one-off transactional interactions.[70] Lives lived on social media are superficial and filled with quickly adopted and then dispensed-with relationships, where attention (and "likes") matter more than reciprocity and depth. To heal as a society and to better serve those who are most in need, we have to build systems that support extended, deep, and mutual relationships. Botticelli quotes MIT social scientist Sherry Turkle:

> Turkle sees us increasingly turning away from the rigors of real-time, face-to-face relationships and leaning into what she believes are the simpler and more superficial forms of connection available through cyberspace. "We expect more from technology and less from each other" (p. xii), she writes.[71]

My original question for this book was, Can higher education learn to love its students again? I came to ask that question of the wide range of other helping, people-focused professions and sectors. Students need to be loved by their teachers. Patients need to be loved by their caregivers.

Clients need to be loved by their therapists and counselors. The incarcerated need to be loved by their jailers. At least, loved in the sense of mattering, lifting up, mutuality, and sustained commitment.

That can only happen with human beings—not systems, technology, or policies. Our needs are so massive and our systems so broken that we can only fix them by flooding them with people who are paid enough, cared for enough, supported enough—dare I say loved enough—to extend all of that care to those who need it the most. What we know of such work and of human need is that the healing will be as much for the caregivers as for those receiving care. The HWI is a way of making that happen, but it requires a radical rethinking of work—a rethinking that I am convinced will be forced upon us.

In the meantime, all who lead and who share a sense that we are too broken, that capitalism, at least as we have known it, has eroded our democracy and broken the spirit of too many of our fellow citizens, perhaps even ourselves—we have an opportunity to rethink the work, rethink the organizations we lead, and find ways to put human relations back at the center of things. That effort begins by looking inward and examining our own leadership practices, the subject of our next and final chapter.

THE HEART OF LEADERSHIP

Almost everyone I met in the learner's journey that led to this book believes we live in a broken world and that our redemption lies in human relationships, the most basic existential power of making people feel like they matter, investing in their growth, and hearing their story. I write during a pandemic, when biological forces afflict our species. But the pandemic that began before the coronavirus and will persist after it subsides or becomes endemic is the pandemic of despair, which has led to emergency levels of depression, suicide, self-medication through alcohol and drugs, political violence, and nihilism. While global, the pandemic of despair is most dramatically manifest in the United States, where the perpetual tension between community and individualism has emphatically swung away from a sense of shared community and identity, a loss of what NYU psychoanalyst Jessica Benjamin calls thirdness, the psychic space where we see each other, forgive each other, and cover each other's back—the place of common good.

The sources? Capitalism, certainly, which has fetishized shareholder value and short-term return over the interests of employees, customers, communities, and, most dangerously, the planet. Social media, too, which has made us more connected and lonelier than before, creating myopic echo chambers of thinking and misinformation that divide rather than unite us. Social media is a ready platform for the worst traits in human nature, from perversity to political demagoguery. Globalization, which has lifted millions out of abject poverty but has moved our worst environmental and human abuses down a fragile supply chain (as was amply demonstrated during the pandemic) out of sight, and has made *cheap* more important than *quality*, encouraging a throwaway consumerism. Taken together, those forces have produced on a grand scale the alienation and psychic disassociation described by writers such as D. H. Lawrence and J. D. Salinger, sociologists like Émile Durkheim, Max Weber, and Frantz Fanon, and philosophers such as Marx and Hegel.

Perhaps we need to be this broken to move from incrementalism, political gridlock, and slow change to the kind of fundamental change we need to save our planet and our people. CEOs like Michael H. McCain, leader of multibillion-dollar Canadian company Maple Leaf Foods, are writing:

> Leading this effort cannot be confined to government, NGOs or social activists. It can only succeed with the direct engagement of forward-thinking business leaders. Yes, capitalism is in peril, and requires revolutionary thinking. Change begins with a new vision for the future. Some might face this prospect with denial, cynicism, or fear. I think it offers hope for a sustainable and equitable path forward—and hope is always inspiring.[1]

Howard Brodsky said, "Capitalism, as we know it, is broken, with increasing wealth inequity, and an increase not only of financial poverty, but poverty of hope." We can only address the massive challenge before us with new systems and organizations that respect and ennoble people, that replace tired and failing models and structures with frameworks and entities like the earlier described public benefit companies, contemporary cooperatives, and organizations that meld the best traits of for-profit and nonprofits, public and private.

These are choices we can make, and in exploring this topic I met one leader after another rethinking the way they serve people. They describe with insight and sophistication the redesign of systems, incentives, financial models, regulatory frameworks, organizational dynamics and culture, and capital markets. In every case I was struck by their intelligence. More than that, I was struck by their values—values largely shaped by their upbringing, including a strong responsibility to care for others and the welfare of the collective.

Howard is a beloved figure at CCA Global and in his local community, and like many of those I interviewed, he has a deeply empathetic nature and is a caretaker of people. He is the type of person who can fire someone, and the person will actually feel better afterward than they did before that fateful conversation and process. He recalls that as a twenty-eight-year-old entrepreneur, he had hired an industrial psychologist, Lester Tobias, to improve hiring and the working relationships of people in his still-young company. Tobias insisted on an exhaustive analysis of Howard as a first step.

Howard recalls, "He told me that unless my business produced values that are socially successful, where the world is better for what we were doing, I would not be happy or fulfilled." He says the source of that ethos lies in his Jewish heritage and his upbringing, especially the influence of his mother (his father died young). As he shared that background with me, he paused for a few moments and said, "I feel badly for those who never have enough, who have more than they or their kids could ever spend in a lifetime and still it's not enough. I don't believe many of them are happy people and this is part of what is breaking capitalism."

Howard and others I interviewed are willing to say they have enough to pay more in taxes, both personal and corporate. Rachel Carlson says:

> We might say that profits over $1 billion or $10 billion a year should be taxed at an escalating rate, that incomes at $1 million should be taxed more than incomes of $100,000. Some might say I am arguing against my self-interest, but I want to live in a functioning and equitable society with functioning capital markets.

Both argue that philanthropy and nonprofits are solving the public- and private-sector failures. Rachel says, "I'm actually happier when I'm paying taxes because I actually believe that government is often a better distributor of those funds than philanthropy, which is so often an expression of ego." Both argue for new models of doing business, but ones that link entrepreneurial success and business goals to social values in order to support the community, the environment, and the idea "that everyone needs to do well, not just the lucky few," to use Howard's phrase.

Both Howard and Rachel are entrepreneurs, embrace economic growth, and have reaped material rewards from their work, as I have in mine. Not one of us is an ascetic, giving up all material possessions to serve humanity. Yet they are committed to sharing those rewards, possess a core respect for other human beings, and feel some call of service to others.

In the opening of this book, I talked about the values learned from my parents and a sense of complicity developed in my Catholic upbringing, the deeply rooted sense that the decisions we make have moral implications, that those decisions can be good for others or self-serving at others' expense, and that we all exist in a connectedness that became startlingly clear during the pandemic.

In her extraordinary *Finding the Mother Tree: Discovering the Wisdom of the Forest*, forest ecologist Suzanne Simard describes the once controversial and now widely accepted revelation that trees in a forest communicate, take care of each other, signal warning, and care for their young—a form of sentience not so different from ours—through "a web of interdependence, linked by a system of underground channels, where they perceive and connect and relate with an ancient intricacy and wisdom that can no longer be denied."[2] She describes her early struggle to understand why plantation trees, the seedlings planted after timber companies clear-cut a forest, were struggling and dying. She noticed that healthy trees and plants had roots fully covered with a wide variety of fungal membranes, part of a mycorrhizal network that some have dubbed the wood-wide network.[3] The seedlings were unconnected, not part of a larger society of trees taking care of each other, finding communal health in their interconnectedness, "wired for wisdom, sentience, and healing," as Simard says.[4] At the heart of such forests are the oldest and largest trees, what she calls the mother trees, mothering the whole.[5] It is a kind of love.

Love is a word that we do not often use in our discussions of leadership. We hint at it sometimes when we talk about someone's emotional intelligence or empathy, but it feels too imprecise or squishy or new age. Yet when we think about the highest stakes leadership, people leading others in combat, where lives depend on the leader's skills, the single most important attribute of the leader is not courage nor tactical creativity nor technical skills. It's love.

Researchers studying the character traits of leaders at the US Military Academy at West Point found that "love predicts accomplishments as a leader."[6] Howard is unabashed in talking about love in his work, saying,

I always say I process an issue from my mind, but the decision comes from my heart. If you have love in your decision-making . . . it's powerful. We had a member recently retire and he wrote me a beautiful letter about what our organization meant to him and his family and his kids. He said, "You built a business of love." Actually, I've had multiple people in the company use that phrase, that this company was built on love. I think it's caring. It's not that you're not concerned about profit, but that people come before profit, and that there's a capacity to lead from the heart, not just the mind, and that you care about them, not just that they'll be productive in your environment, but they're going to be productive in their own life—that you'll care for them is much greater than just what it does for your own economic means as a company.

If there is one consistent theme characterizing our worst leaders it is lovelessness in their practice and, almost always, lovelessness in their upbringing. Adolf Hitler suffered a cruel and domineering father, as did Donald Trump, whose father, Fred, taught the future president that the world was made up of winners and losers.[7] While they are dramatic examples, our politics and business worlds are populated with leaders who love few and none more than themselves. The worst of them amass billions, fight to hold every penny, and confuse their ability to innovate with virtue.

More than one combat veteran has told me that the opposite of fear is not bravery, but love. Wil Zemp, winner of the Distinguished Service Cross for an engagement in Afghanistan in which his actions would seem like overblown fiction if depicted in a movie, told me he had never been more frightened, but that he had to act for his men. It was when Emma, our first child, entered the world and the doctor asked me to cut the umbilical cord that I had the almost mystical sense of selflessness that marked the start of parenthood. The moment repeated two-and-a-half years later when Hannah, our second daughter, was born. In those moments I experienced something much scarier than death to me: that any harm should befall these tiny beings with whom I had been acquainted all of thirty seconds.

The opposite of that fear is love. I had sat through countless Catholic masses growing up and heard this phrase from John 3:16 many times—"For God so loved the world that He gave His one and only Son"—and it barely registered. I was more likely to be thinking about my hockey game later that day or how the Celtics would do against the Lakers. However, when I heard that phrase during mass after I had become a parent, it floored me, and I understood the symbolic power of sacrifice greater than the unthinkable.

I've talked to young friends who share that they might start a family, and I have to restrain myself because I know I can sound like a born-again Christian saying they found Jesus and everything changed. Instead, I tell them that the experience is so profound that the pro and con list Pat and I had constructed before kids (Pros: need no excuse to re-watch Disney movies, someone to take care of us in our old age, fun to dress them up; Cons: less disposable income, diapers, no spontaneous adventures, adolescence, expense of college . . . the list went on at some length) was immediately rendered meaningless one minute into parenthood. One of the people with whom I discussed the subject recently emailed me and wrote:

> Three-and-half years ago . . . you, Scott and I were exchanging emails, and I had asked for your advice with the birth of our first child. You mentioned that fatherhood was "the best thing you'll ever do." Perhaps Covid quarantine is getting to me, but as we expect #3, I wanted to thank you for that advice and for the SNHU time which has helped me to be the best I can for my family.

I read somewhere that those without children are happier than those with them. Parenting brings no lack of sleepless nights, anxiety, and other unhappiness, that's for sure. There have been so many moments of boundless joy and mirth as well. But neither of those are the point, it seems to me. It is that there are other humans that mean more to me than me, that my heart is no longer mine, that their vulnerabilities are mine as well.

When we can extend that love to those with whom we work and those we serve—and yes, I know we don't usually call it love, preferring *duty* or *service*—we build different kinds of organizations. That difference is reflected in culture and the behavioral norms that are then accepted or rejected within an organization or system. While the system is always smarter than its leadership, especially if we know how to harness the experience, intelligence, and creativity that sit throughout a system and often most abundantly with those closest to the work, culture is most powerfully shaped by leadership.

In writing about military leadership, Army veteran and historian Doug Meyer says, "Love, passion, passio, agape, compassion—whatever word we use, our soldiers will never care what we know until they know we care."[8] That caring then translates into unit cohesion and a willingness to give all for the mission.

In the late 1940s, sociologists Edward Shils and Morris Janowitz puzzled over why the German Army had continued to stubbornly fight for so long after all was lost, and they concluded, "A soldier continued to fight well beyond the point when the battle or war was lost as long as the group possessed leadership with which he could identify himself, and as long as he gave affection to and received affection from the other members of his squad or platoon."[9]

The culture of firefighters is to run into the burning building, to run toward, not away from danger. During the pandemic, we saw medical professionals doing heroic work and paying an enormous price because the culture of care is so important that they will risk their lives to take care of patients, even those who have endangered their lives and the lives of caregivers by refusing to get a simple vaccine. The culture at SNHU is that we do everything we can to help students succeed in a culture of care. My job as a leader is to nurture the culture that makes that happen when no one else is watching, when people have choices. As Frances Frei and Anne Morriss, authors of *Unleashed: The Unapologetic Leader's Guide to Empowering Everyone Around You* and the team that was brought in to help Uber recover from its calamitous breakdown in leadership and culture, write:

> Your job as a leader is to create the conditions for the people around you to become increasingly effective, to help them realize their capacity and power. And not only when you are in the trenches with them, but also when you are not around, and even (this is the cleanest test) after you've permanently moved from the team.[10]

When we get it wrong—and we do sometimes—I almost always find a disconnect between our mission and culture and the actions of our people involved, and often the broken link is the leadership of that group within our organization. Not because they are uncaring or ill intended, but because they have prioritized something other than the well-being of those we serve. My favorite moments as a leader are when I hear stories of our staff going beyond what is merely expected to help a student. That's when I know our culture is working and our leaders are leading with care and service.

Oftentimes, the best predictor of their efficacy is how they spend their time, what gets most of their attention. In all our human-helping work, people want to be seen, to know they matter, to be understood, to have their stories heard, and to know we are with them to make them better, whether they are learners, patients, inmates, or employees. That takes time and it takes patience with the messiness that comes with each and every human being.

As examined in the previous chapter, time and messiness run counter to the efficiency and orderly processes that scaled systems crave. To build scaled systems that keep humans and the time they require at the center of things, we need new organizational and system models. In my work to understand the challenge of rehumanizing our caregiving work, from K–12 to eldercare, I spent time with creative leaders who are attempting to build scalable systems that respect and support and know the individuals they serve. Whether the health coaches that Alexander Packard employs at One Medical, the primacy of counselors in the Groups Recover Together model, the holistic understanding of student support that Sara Goldrick-Rab brings to the work of the Hope Center, or SNHU's focus on academic coaches, all scaled solutions to very human challenges happen in relationships. Relationships require time, sustained commitment, and require the caregiver—whether teacher, counselor, physician, or prison guard—to give of themselves. It's a lot to ask.

At SNHU we enroll thousands of students who work in health care, many in frontline clinical roles. During the pandemic, their conversations with our academic coaches often started with questions about their academic work or what course they would take in the next term but increasingly turned to their traumas and stories of people dying in numbers they had never encountered before, often alone, and their own fear of a disease that we were still struggling to understand. They shared those stories with our academic advisers, with whom they have a kind of intimacy, so they wouldn't need to share them with their own loved ones. It took a toll, and the staff who lead our advising teams spent more and more time caring for them and supporting them.

Sara Goldrick-Rab was intrigued by the coaching at InsideTrack, a company that works on improving student persistence, and asked to listen in on the calls they made. She says:

> The calls are brilliant. These folks know exactly how to talk to students. When I explored why, it's in large part because every single one of them gets coaching every week. Not management. Coaching. And I was so amazed that the coaches get coaches. In most of education, you have faculty and administrators who are not processing with anybody, not at all, totally in isolation and dealing with humans and the full breadth of their humanity, and frankly, that is very painful in many ways. What my team deals with by knowing what we know, and what I deal with by walking into a classroom and knowing the burdens my students carry, because my eyes are open, it is a heavy experience. I cannot shrug a student off. I have to take a lot more time to do what I do.

The "full breadth of their humanity" is what we must embrace if we are to genuinely engage in relationships, and that takes time, support, and a willingness to think of those we serve in the kind of holistic work Sara describes.

Many of my worst moments as a leader have come when I've put the system—the rules, the processes, the organizational goals—before people. I like order and things to run smoothly so I can easily default to the system because that is efficient, whereas the people part is so often messy, time-consuming, and requires more from me.

I'm still pained to think about the case of Tom B., a longtime leader on my team, who failed to land a high-potential employer partner who could have brought thousands of students to us, helping us reach more students while lowering our operating cost and helping the bottom line. As I listened to his account of what went wrong, I was increasingly certain that he had made mistakes in his approach and had become impatient with what sounded like rationalization to me. When he left my office, I called my contacts at the employer, asked if I could come visit, and a few days later flew to their headquarters. I got the discussions back on track, and we soon landed the partnership. That was leadership in action, I told myself.

It was failed leadership. While landing that partnership was good for SNHU, I had sidelined Tom B. Convinced he didn't "get it," I left him out of the problem-solving process, the trip, and the success story. I spent no time with him unpacking what had happened, how he might have approached matters differently, or what role he could play in saving the deal. Indeed, when we announced the partnership, he not only couldn't share in the success, but he also had the sense that everyone else knew he had failed.

I didn't leave Tom out to punish him. It was more thoughtless than that as I focused on our organizational need to get that partnership, considering not at all how he might learn or feel about not being included. In *Unleashed*, Frei and Morriss define leadership as "empowering other people as a result of your presence—and making sure that continues in your absence."[11] I did neither for Tom B., and I later apologized to him in front of my whole team. It was hard for me to admit my thoughtlessness, and it made everyone squirm a little in their seats. As Tom listened, his eyes welled up with tears. He sought me out afterward and thanked me. While we repaired our relationship and he remains a friend, he not long after that episode left our organization.

On another occasion, a relatively new leader was struggling with Sally (not her real name), one of our longtime employees, someone who had done really important work for us and had led a number of key

THE HEART OF LEADERSHIP

initiatives. The new leader, let's call her Ronnie, came to me and said, "I've decided to fire Sally." I was troubled by the decision, had a growing conviction that Ronnie was a poor manager of people, and while I could see the ways Sally had not acquitted herself well with her new boss, I worried about how we were treating her. I asked Sally to meet with me, and she was pretty awful in our meeting, angry at how Ronnie was treating her, probably afraid, and feeling disrespected given all her previous accomplishments. Sally wasn't the person I had always known in that moment. So I did the easy thing and bowed to our system's reporting lines and Ronnie's authority to fire Sally despite my unease.

Months later we came to realize Ronnie's shortcomings and moved her into another role, got her a lot of coaching, and made sure she wasn't managing people. But Sally had paid the price. In this case, I didn't just put the system first, I did so to avoid the time and work it would have taken to take better care of Sally.

Later, when we heard that Sally was still not working and had been diagnosed with a life-threatening disease, I reached out to Amelia Manning, my chief operating officer, and said, "I've never felt good about what happened to Sally and now she is in real trouble. I want to hire her back and help her out." Amelia agreed, sharing my sense that we had failed Sally. I met Sally for lunch and apologized, telling her that I had let her down, asking her to come back to work for us. Like Tom, she cried—with relief, certainly, given her circumstances, but also because there was redemption in the moment.

In both Tom's and Sally's cases, doing the right thing would have required me to put in time, to navigate their struggles, work with them to understand what was not working and then to fix it. It would also have been risky. There was a chance that Tom would fail again or impede our ability to get the partnership talks sorted out. There was a chance that Ronnie was right, that Sally would not get over her indignation and remain recalcitrant, or that Ronnie, an important new leader (whatever my growing misgivings) would feel that I had undercut her in this early test of our relationship. Organizational needs and processes allowed me to avoid the risks and the messiness and the time-consuming work of, well, leadership.

In my role leading a large organization, my calling is to care for the people who work for us and the people we serve. No one is less or more deserving of my care because of their title or their job or their performance as a student. No one is less important as a person, even if jobs differ in their impact or import and some students are stars and others are absolutely maddening. Everyone matters.

Similarly, as an educator my calling is to care for all of our students. I say that with a kind of certainty, but I get it wrong sometimes. When the pandemic hit, I knew I needed to be more attentive to people's needs, to be more present, and to think through the impact on our students. The pandemic made those needs obvious and urgent, but in attending to that work, a more subtle thing happened. I was reminded that I am most fulfilled and feel most impactful not in business class travel to one meeting or conference or another, not by taking the stage somewhere, or in a meeting with some really important person, but by taking good care of my organization, the people in it, and the people it serves.

That's not a paternal act of charity or benevolence from on high. It means the opposite: giving power to others, learning together in a world utterly changed, building a network instead of a hierarchy, giving rather than gaining. Jung said that we cannot discover self at the top of the mountain, but only in community.[12] There is paradox in that notion. We find and know ourselves in community, not in opposition to it.

I opened this book with my own story and my Acadian background, growing up in a culture that resists systems but thrives in community. As a result, while I am quick to find what doesn't work in our current systems and seek to innovate, I remain unwavering in my conviction that our work must be for the greater good, for the community.

This book started with the question of whether higher education can learn to love its students again and expanded to look at other caregiving or nurturing systems and expanded again to look at our society writ large. If we are to heal as a planet, as a species, as a society, as individuals, we have to be learners again and revisit the wisdom found in the trees, in indigenous cultures, in our faith traditions, and in the moments when we have been at our best, lifting up individuals, building teams, creating community, and contributing to the greater good. I've learned that lesson from my parents and family, from teachers, and in an education system that did love its students. At least it seemed to love me.

When Hannah was considering doctoral programs, she had offers from some of the most elite universities in the country (as my high school friends say, "She's got her mother's brains and her father's height."). I was driving somewhere with the president of one of those institutions discussing her options, and he said that Hannah shouldn't come here, even though the university would love to have her. But it's not a kind place, he said. He went on to describe an elite faculty that left the places that had nurtured and supported them for the allure of his school and its reputation. He said, "These are people who left the places that helped them become successful. They use their graduate students to support their own work and most will claim any accolades. We tell them they are the best at what they do and they mostly act like it—huge egos."

It was a startling admission and at once resonated. I was lucky to do my doctoral work with a great mentor, Charlie Moran, a professor at the University of Massachusetts in Amherst. I was exploring the use of technology in writing, then a new development, and Charlie joined me as a co-learner more than expert supervisor. When we published or presented together, he made sure my name came first ("That's the way it is in the alphabet and so it shall be here," he used to say to me), and he cared for me as a person as well as a graduate student. My dissertation director, Anne Herrington, very much did the same, and I contrast the care and support I received with the experience of my daughters, who attended more elite universities, and my colleague's "it is not a kind place" comment.

My experience was kinder. It was loving. I worked with people genuinely committed to lifting me up and discovering my potential, not only as an academic, but also as a human being. I mattered to them, they expected more of me, they took the time to know me and to hear my stories, and however much the system in which they worked encouraged or discouraged it, they measured at least some portion of their success by my success.

As an organization, we do not want to be a for-profit. We want to be for-love. What a thing to write. But the greatest lesson I have learned is that I have done my best work for love, and I see that every day around me as well. I've also learned that there is no real separation between my private and work lives. I am who I am at work because of who I've been as a son, a student, a husband, a father, and a friend. There is no life and work balance—there is just life. A bad day at work bleeds right into home life that evening. An unhappy life at home will shape the day at work. We bring our whole selves, our heads and hearts and the sum of our experience, to each.

Love takes many forms, but in each we are lifted outside of ourselves to become part of something bigger. I am an individual, but as a member of my family, my Acadian clan, my community, my university, my country, I can be so much more elevated as a human being.

There is in early twentieth-century literature an obsession with a fragmented world and the possibility of meaning and pulling the whole together, if only momentarily. In James Joyce's *Portrait of the Artist as a Young Man*, this happens almost as mystical epiphanies—a sense of the wholeness of things beyond rationality, often sparked by everyday things.

Similarly, in Robert Frost's poem "Mending Wall," with its often misinterpreted line, "Good fences make good neighbors," the annual repair and resetting of the wall is what brings together the two very different men in the poem. It's about connectivity with other human beings, about their mattering to us and our mattering to them—whether as family, friends, neighbors, students, or coworkers—and if there is any hope for this broken world, it will be through our sense of complicity and connection, that we owe something to each other that can only be found in relationships, not transactions.

Some years ago, I asked my board of trustees to have dinner with me and arranged a private room at a local restaurant. Our organization was at one of those key inflection points in terms of its growth and scale, talent, and systems. For the next phase in its evolution, I knew we would need to make large investments in new systems and processes, expand into new program offerings, consider what we'd stop doing, and reassess our leadership team. Starting with me. When everyone had their food in front of them and their wine glasses full, I said to them:

I'm pretty proud of what we have built together and my role in it, but I don't know if I am the right leader for this next phase. I'm still trying to understand what will be required of my role and if I'm the right guy to do it. If I'm not, I want to figure that out before you do and be the one who says it out loud.

My board has always been supportive, rushed to say reassuring things, and with their usual kindness resolved to help in any way they could. We did most of what we set out to do in that next phase of growth, and by most measures have been successful. We are at another inflection point now. With the pandemic, the world has changed, as have our students and our employees. Behaviors, needs, and expectations are different. Threats and opportunities present themselves more rapidly than ever before. I'm pretty sure that the organization we built for the last two decades is not the right organization for the next five, ten, or more years. Our mission remains the same, to transform lives at scale, and in this time of growing inequality and uncertainty, where the lack of a postsecondary credential almost guarantees a life of deprivation and struggle (even if having that credential is no promise of success), our work has never been more important.

How we do that work must change, which means that my leadership is again in question. I've learned so much from the many inspiring people I've spent time with while writing this book. My personal manifesto, offered to you, dear reader, and promised to the organization I lead, is as follows:

- To keep learning, ask more questions, collect more stories. While I remain clear about our mission and will use it to keep us honest, I have to find new ways to do the work in a new world in which certainty is dangerous. The most powerful stories and learning will come from those we serve and the people closest to the work. In our leadership meetings and in my own discourse, I must listen for the questions and the curiosity and the stories that make us uncomfortable.
- To look at our systems and our organization through the lens of mattering. Simply, do the structures we have built for

serving people make them feel like they matter, that we know them? We need to imagine new systems and structures that can better ensure our care for people and those we serve. Many of those mentioned in this book are reimagining the systems they created—with all the external constraints working against them—and refusing to accept systems and ways of doing the work that are increasingly ineffective and often dehumanizing.

- To hire and develop leaders who are more empathetic than expert. While we want expertise, of course, we need leaders—including me—who put people first, our students first, and whose intrinsic motivation is love, complicity, and service. We need to embrace that our role as leaders is to create leaders and empower people at every level. We have so often hired people for whom we have said, "They aren't really great in terms of emotional intelligence, but they are so damn good at the work that we can work with them on the people part." It never works. It never, ever works.

- To measure our well-being by the well-being of the whole. It's not enough to say my family and I are doing fine. To say that my team is doing well. To say that my organization is doing great. To report our good Net Promoter Scores from students. We have to ask about all of those whose lives we touch, including the students who are not successful, the unhappy employees, the vendors from whom we purchase (and their people), our local community, and more.

When Maasai warriors greet each other, they often say, "*Eserian nakera*," which means, "How are the children?" The response is typically, "All the children are well," even if neither warrior actually has children. The exchange is about the well-being of the whole community. If all the children are well—fed, safe, nurtured, happy—then all else has to be going well. The question is an invitation to think beyond oneself.

- To not shortchange time with the people that need me. To be effective in this very human work we do is to be relational, not transactional, and that requires sustained, deep commitment and a willingness to stay with the messiness that is human relations. My impatience, sense of urgency around the needs we are addressing, and desire for orderliness often drives the work but has not always served my people well. Much of the most important work we will need to do going forward can't be rushed, and sometimes we have to go slower to go faster. A lesson I'm learning.

I need to be better, more imaginative, and diligent on all points of this manifesto. As a leader, I make trade-offs every day, ask people to do hard things, grapple with problems and all the messiness of human nature. Sometimes that means holding people accountable and even saying "no more." Leaders are responsible for allocating resources, and when we have multiple stakeholders and only so much money, we often have to make trade-offs. That requires wisdom, insight, and integrity, and yet none of those qualities matter much if they are not filtered through the emotional chambers of the heart.

The leaders who are working to rethink our human-centered systems almost always have walked the path of those they seek to serve or have seen their needs close up. Colleen Nicewicz of Groups Recover Together says, "What brought me here was, first and foremost and like so many of our staff, personal connections to addiction in my family and my husband's family." Sara Goldrick-Rab talks about the violence and abuse in her youth and the ways the schools she attended failed to see her struggles and pain, even when explicitly expressed in her own behavior. They never sought out her stories. While Sara had trauma and physical violence in her home, she also had the earlier mentioned grandparents and family members to admire and act as role models. She is now an ardent champion of knowing underserved students in holistic ways that require grappling with whatever trauma and deprivation they carry.

Ken Oliver spent twenty-four years in prison, nine of them in solitary confinement, and experienced the humiliation and dehumanization not only of those years inside but also in the process of reentry. Lorris Betz saw the dehumanizing treatment of his wife in the healthcare system he actually led and resolved to take a closer look and start the changes he needed to make. Arne Duncan describes his mother's work in the poorest and most dangerous parts of Chicago, offering after-school programs to kids navigating gangs, poverty, and violence, and providing them safety, learning, and, most importantly, hope.

Similarly, my work has its roots in the way my parents led their lives and the direct transformational power of teachers—from sixth grade through doctorate—who cared about me as a student and, more importantly, as a person. They helped an immigrant kid with little means and modest aspirations (part of me still wants to be a firefighter or cop), and changed the whole trajectory of my life and thus the lives of our daughters. If "hurt people hurt people," as is commonly observed, I like to think that helped people help others and that like those just mentioned, I do this work in higher education because I've seen the power of higher education to so powerfully change my life for the better.

I often tell my story at the opening of presentations or keynote speeches before setting out on my critique of where higher education has evolved, the ways it fails too many, and the need to fix the broken system. Afterward, there is almost always a line of people who want to talk with me and share that they, too, were first generation, that college changed their lives, and that they are frustrated at the ways their experience is now out of reach of too many.

While our systems may be broken, our people are not.

Our K–12 schools, health-care systems, mental health providers, social service agencies, criminal justice systems, refugee programs, governments, and universities are filled with people who yearn for something better. The needs are enormous, the solutions have to be scaled to meet the need, but the starting point for all those who lead the effort is in the hopes and needs, the messy mystery of the individual human heart. The one that beats in our chest as a leader and the one that beats in the chest of the person we hope to lift up into a better life.

ACKNOWLEDGMENTS

M y original working title for this book was *A Learner's Journey*, and while the title eventually changed, the project was very much a learning journey for me—one of the best I've experienced. The best learning came from my hours spent in conversation with the remarkable people I interviewed along the way. They inspired me with their intelligence, generosity, and big hearts, and made me their student in the best of ways. In my writing, I came back again and again to the work of **Dr. Lorris Betz**, former CEO of University of Utah Health, who cares so deeply about patients and respecting their humanity. Similarly, **Dr. Matt Biel**, chief of child and adolescent psychiatry and pediatrics at Georgetown University Medical Center, has a huge heart, and, if I could, I'd put the world's children under his care. **Howard Brodsky**, cofounder, chairman, and co-CEO of CCA Global Partners, speaks unabashedly about love and leadership, and it is fitting that he features so prominently in the last chapter. How have I gone so long and not known about the work of **Dr. Jessica Benjamin** at New York University, who patiently walked me through her concept of "thirdness," a framework that our country so desperately needs in order to heal? **Rachel Carson**, founder and CEO of Guild Education, wants to reinvent capitalism and we all need her to succeed—she has the brains and heart to do it. I had the privilege of working for former **US Secretary of Education Arne Duncan**, and my conversations with him simply reaffirm for me what I've long known: that few people care more about or put their time into the hardest work in the hardest places than Arne. He is the real deal. I've known **Dr. Greg Elliott**, professor of sociology at Brown University, for a long time now, and his work on "mattering" has deeply informed my thinking and my approach to education and leadership. Students have no more fierce a champion than **Sara Goldrick-Rab**, founder of the Hope Center for College Community and Justice and a professor of sociology and medicine at Temple University. My old friend **Dennis Littky**, cofounder of The Metropolitan School and College Unbound, is the single most committed and passionate educator I know and remains an inspiration to me. On a dark night in a remote refugee camp, **Ignazio Matteini** of the United Nations High Commissioner for Refugees helped me understand how hope sustains even amidst so much inhumanity. He is a good man. **Emily McCann**, former CEO of Citizen Schools, combines a fine business mind and deep respect for every child as an individual. **Colleen Nicewicz**, CEO of Groups Recover Together, similarly starts with the humanity and respect of every client and is rethinking care with a focus on people first. I know few people who could endure the torture of years in solitary confinement, and then prison, and come out the other side in the way that **Ken Oliver** has done. Now directing philanthropy for the HR tech company Chekr, he is an astounding person. **Alexander Packard**, former president of Iora Health system and current chief integration officer at One Medical, gives me hope that we can genuinely reinvent scaled, complicated systems that put people at the center of things. **Dr. Matt Steinfeld**, assistant professor of psychiatry at Yale School of Medicine, helped me remember that all progress, healing, and leadership happens in relationship with others. I could have spent days with each of these remarkable people, devoted a whole chapter (maybe a book) to each of them, and remain infinitely grateful for their contributions to my understanding and work. The world is a much better place that they are in it.

No one should believe the myth of the solitary writer. I had a small but powerful circle of readers who cheered me on and also demanded more of me as they read draft chapters. My wife, Pat, remains my compass. No one has a better bullshit meter, a more genuine sense of fairness and justice, and abiding interest and appreciation for others. Whenever she read something, arched one eyebrow, and asked, "Really . . . ?" I knew it was time to revise. Margaret Moffett is a wonderful writer in her own right and helped me get the structure down, stay true to my voice, tighten up the language, and debrief the many interviews she joined me in conducting. She also brought conviction to this project, and her belief in the book bolstered mine when I was not so sure. I want her at my side for any and all future books . . . if she could bear me for another project. Kemp Battle is a writer, editor, and thought partner, and he often held on to a clearer vision for this book than even I, its author, could possess. He is a wise friend and a caring person, and he is unwilling to settle for the superficial. He knows this life is too precious to be so wasted. They were demanding readers in the best sense, often knowing and seeing better versions of what I had written when I could not. Whatever is good and valuable in this book owes a lot to the three of them. Meaghan Rajkumar provided valuable support in chasing down references and documenting sources—always cheerfully and accompanied by an encouraging note. This was my dream team.

ACKNOWLEDGMENTS

When I pitched this book to agents, one asked me about my imagined audience, and I said that I was writing with my daughters Emma and Hannah in mind. She dismissed that notion, suggesting that I write them a letter instead. Yet throughout the writing process, I used them as a compass and test of my thinking. Yes, this book is written for a wide audience, but no audience matters more to me than my two remarkable daughters. They give me hope for the world.

I am grateful to Matt Holt, my publisher at BenBella Books. He fought for this book and rallied his team around it, and by being such a believer made me one as well. Katie Dickman was my developmental editor and shepherded the process, while Ruth Strother was an astoundingly careful copy editor who improved my writing. Brigid Pearson, who designed the cover, made my life difficult with more than one great choice. My thanks also go to Mallory Hyde and the rest of the marketing team. The hope of all writers is that readers can come to know of their books, and the BenBella marketing team worked hard to tell my story.

The book begins with my own story and is, in many ways, a love letter to my parents, Eugene and Delphine. They rarely *talked* about love for others. They didn't have to—they lived it every day, in ways big and small. They treated everyone with respect, shared all they had, and walked through the world with a "there but for the grace of God go I" compassion for others. Good Acadians that they were, they also loved a good laugh, valued a good story, looked askance at superiority or entitlement, were generous with a pour, and knew that the kitchen table is where relationships best happen. On Saturday mornings, when my mother's homemade bread was coming out of the oven, filling the house with that delicious smell, friends and family would pass through one after another, each knowing that at my parents' table they were

ACKNOWLEDGMENTS

the most important person in the world. I have written this book to explore how we build systems and organizations that make the people they serve feel that same way, devoting a lot of hours to research, interviews, and thinking to arrive at what my parents always knew and never had to think about: that other people matter most, and everyone deserves respect, dignity, and a helping hand when in need. This is, in many ways, their book.

NOTES

Introduction

1. Rama Apoorva, "Trends in Health Care Spending," *American Medical Association*, accessed December 23, 2021, https://www.ama-assn.org /about/research/trends-health-care-spending.

2. Peter Wagner and Bernadette Rabuy, "Following the Money of Mass Incarceration," Prison Policy Initiative, January 25, 2017, https://www .prisonpolicy.org/reports/money.html.

3. "Fast Facts: Expenditures, National Center for Education Statistics, accessed December 23, 2021, https://nces.ed.gov/fastfacts/display.asp ?id=75.

4. Emma Findlen LeBlanc, "Precarity and Persistence in Canada's Company Province" (doctoral dissertation, University of Oxford, 2018), 77–78.

5. Clara Marburg Kirk and Rudolph Kirk, *William Dean Howells: Representative Selections, with Introduction, Bibliography, and Notes* (New York: American Book Company, 1950), cxiii.

6. Board of Governors of the Federal Reserve System, *Report on the Economic Well-Being of U.S. Households in 2018*, May 2019, https://www .federalreserve.gov/publications/files/2018-report-economic-well -being-us-households-201905.pdf.

Mattering

1. Aaron E. Carroll, "To Be Sued Less, Doctors Should Consider Talking to Patients More," *New York Times*, June 1, 2015, https://www.nytimes.com/2015/06/02/upshot/to-be-sued-less-doctors-should-talk-to-patients-more.html.

2. Gregory C. Elliott, *Family Matters: The Importance of Mattering to Family in Adolescence* (Chichester, UK: John Wiley & Sons), 2009.

3. Heather Long, Alyssa Fowers, and Andrew Van Dam, "Why America Has 8.4 Million Unemployed When There Are 10 Million Job Openings, *Washington Post*, September 4, 2021, https://www.washingtonpost.com/business/2021/09/04/ten-million-job-openings-labor-shortage.

4. James Gilligan, *Violence: Reflections on a National Epidemic* (New York: Vintage Books, 1997), 106.

5. Gilligan, 110.

6. Gilligan, 110.

7. Frantz Fanon, *The Wretched of the Earth* (New York: Grove Press, 1968), 124.

8. Simone Weil, "The Iliad, or the Poem of Force," *Chicago Review* 18, no. 2 (1965): 7, https://doi.org/10.2307/25294008.

Dreaming Bigger Dreams

1. Z. Liberman, A. Woodward, and K. Kinzler, "The Origins of Social Categorization (author manuscript)," *Trends in Cognitive Sciences* 21, no. 7 (2017): 556–568, https://www.ncbi.nlm.nih.gov/pmc/articles/PMC5605918.

2. K. Hines Shelvin, R. Rivadeneyra, and C. Zimmerman, "Stereotype Threat in African American Children: The Role of Black Identity and Stereotype Awareness," *Revue Internationale de Psychologie Sociale* 27 (2014): 175–204, https://www.cairn.info/revue-internationale-de-psychologie-sociale-2014-3-page-175.htm.

3. A. M. Cauce, R. Cruz, M. Corona, and R. Conger, "The Face of the Future: Risk and Resilience in Minority Youth," *Nebraska Symposium on Motivation*, 57 (2011): 13–32, https://www.researchgate.net/publication/49691095_The_Face_of_the_Future_Risk_and_Resilience_in_Minority_Youth.

4. Centers for Disease Control and Prevention, "Overdose Deaths Accelerating During COVID-19 (press release)," December 17, 2020, https://www.cdc.gov/media/releases/2020/p1218-overdose-deaths-covid-19.html.

5. "Even Before COVID-19 Pandemic, Youth Suicide Already at Record High," UC Davis Health News, April 8, 2021, https://health.ucdavis.edu/newsroom/news/headlines/even-before-covid-19-pandemic-youth-suicide-already-at-record-high/2021/04.

6. "Refugee Camps," USA for UNHCR, accessed December 23, 2021, https://www.unrefugees.org/refugee-facts/camps/.

7. Gary Hamel and Michele Zanini, *Humanocracy: Creating Organizations as Amazing as the People Inside Them* (Boston: Harvard Business Review Press, 2020), 45.

8. Hamel and Zanini, 43.

9. Hamel and Zanini, 18.

10. Jim Clifton, "The World's Broken Workplace," Gallup News, June 13, 2017, https://news.gallup.com/opinion/chairman/212045/world-broken-workplace.aspx?g_source=position1&g_medium=related&g_campaign=tiles.

11. Adam Chandler, "No, Unemployment Benefits Don't Stop People from Returning to Work," *Washington Post*, May 13, 2021, https://www.washingtonpost.com/outlook/2021/05/13/unemployment-benefits-minimum-wage-work/.

12. David Graeber, *Bullshit Jobs: A Theory* (New York: Simon & Schuster, 2018), 11.

The Power of Stories

1. Radiolab, "Chasing Bugs," WNYC Studios, accessed December 23, 2021, https://www.wnycstudios.org/podcasts/radiolab/articles/91867 -chasing-bugs.
2. Jonathan Gottschall, *The Storytelling Animal: How Stories Make Us Human* (New York: Houghton Mifflin Harcourt, 2013), xiv.
3. Chimamanda Ngozi Adichie, "The Danger of a Single Story," TED video, 2:30, July 2009, https://www.ted.com/talks/chimamanda_ngozi _adichie_the_danger_of_a_single_story?language=en.
4. Adichie, 13:38.
5. Ezra Klein, "Why Does It Have to Be Slaveholders That We Unite Around?" *New York Times*, October 19, 2021, https://www.nytimes .com/2021/10/19/opinion/ezra-klein-podcast-woody-holton.html ?showTranscript=1.
6. Paul Fain, "A College President Breaks Bread with His Foes," *The Chronicle of Higher Education*, August 31, 2009, https://www.chronicle .com/article/a-college-president-breaks-bread-with-his-foes/.
7. Kurt Vonnegut, *Mother Night* (New York: Dell, 1961), v.
8. Jacqueline Novogratz, *Manifesto for a Moral Revolution: Practices to Build a Better World* (New York: St. Martin's Griffin, 2021), 90.
9. Novogratz, 91.
10. Novogratz, 91.

The Problem of Scale

1. "Poverty Facts," PovertyUSA, accessed January 24, 2022, https://www .povertyusa.org/facts.
2. Emma Wager, Jared Ortaliza, and Cynthia Cox, "How Does Health Spending in the U.S. Compare to Other Countries?" Peterson-KFF Health System Tracker, January 21, 2022, https://www.healthsystem tracker.org/chart-collection/health-spending-u-s-compare-countries.

3. "Education Expenditures by Country," National Center for Education Statistics, May 2021, https://nces.ed.gov/programs/coe/indicator/cmd.

4. Jeffrey Selingo, "What Many Have in Common with Scott Walker: College Credits, No Degree," *Washington Post*, February 23, 2015, https://www.washingtonpost.com/news/grade-point/wp/2015/02/23/what-many-have-in-common-with-scott-walker-college-credits-no-degree.

5. "2019 Impact Report," HCA Healthcare, https://hcahealthcareimpact.com/2019-impact-report.pdf.

6. "New Life and New Hope During COVID-19: HCA Healthcare's Commitment to Mothers and Babies," HCA Healthcare, April 28, 2020, https://hcahealthcaretoday.com/2020/04/28/new-life-and-hope-hca-healthcares-commitment-to-mothers-and-babies-during-covid-19/.

7. "HCA Healthcare Reports Fourth Quarter 2020 Results and Provides 2021 Guidance," HCA Healthcare, February 2, 2021, https://investor.hcahealthcare.com/news/news-details/2021/HCA-Healthcare-Reports-Fourth-Quarter-2020-Results-and-Provides-2021-Guidance/default.aspx.

8. Anna Lowenhaupt Tsing, *The Mushroom at the End of the World: On the Possibility of Life in Capitalist Ruins* (Princeton, NJ: Princeton University Press, 2015), 38.

9. Tsing, 38.

10. Jay Rorty, "The Human Cost of Mandatory Minimums," *American Civil Liberties Union* (blog), May 28, 2010, https://www.aclu.org/blog/smart-justice/mass-incarceration/human-cost-mandatory-minimums.

11. Tsing, 197.

12. Tsing, 39.

13. Tsing, 40.

14. "Historical Highest Marginal Income Tax Rates," Tax Policy Center, Urban Institute and Brookings Institution, February 9, 2022, https://www.taxpolicycenter.org/statistics/historical-highest-marginal-income-tax-rates.

15. Kimberly Amadeo, "US Real GDP Growth Rate by Year Compared to Inflation and Unemployment," The Balance, November 10, 2021, https://www.thebalance.com/u-s-gdp-growth-3306008.

16. David Hope and Julian Limberg, "The Economic Consequences of Major Tax Cuts for the Rich," International Inequalities Institute, December 2020, http://eprints.lse.ac.uk/107919/1/Hope_economic _consequences_of_major_tax_cuts_published.pdf.

17. Allan Golston, "For Students the Right Advice Can Make All the Difference," Gates Foundation, May 14, 2018, https://usprogram .gatesfoundation.org/news-and-insights/articles/ps-for-students-the -right-advice-can-make-all-the-difference.

18. Iora Health Find a Location Page, accessed January 25, 2022, https:// www.iorahealth.com/practices/list-of-offices.

19. "One Medical Completes Acquisition of Iora Health," One Medical, September 1, 2021, https://investor.onemedical.com/news-releases /news-release-details/one-medical-completes-acquisition-iora-health.

20. "University of Utah Named Number One Health Care System in Utah," University of Utah Health, July 21, 2015, https://healthcare .utah.edu/publicaffairs/news/2015/07/07-21-15_US_News_rankings .php.

21. Our Organization Page, TED, accessed January 25, 2022, https://www .ted.com/about/our-organization.

22. About Tesla Page, Tesla, accessed January 25, 2022, https://www.tesla .com/ABOUT.

23. Starbucks Mission and Values Page, Starbucks, accessed January 25, 2022, https://stories.starbucks.com/press/2015/starbucks-mission-and -values.

24. New York Public Library NYPL's Mission Statement Page, accessed January 25, 2022, https://www.nypl.org/help/about-nypl/mission.

25. Our Mission Page, Patagonia, accessed January 25, 2022, https://www .patagonia.com.au/pages/our-mission.

26. Mission & Vision Page, Los Angeles Unified School District, accessed January 25, 2022, https://achieve.lausd.net/strategies.

27. Who We Are Page, Amazon, accessed January 25, 2022, https://www.aboutamazon.com/about-us.

28. About University of Utah Hospitals & Clinics Page, University of Utah Health, accessed January 25, 2022, https://healthcare.utah.edu/about.

29. About Our Offices/Leadership Page, Louisiana Department of Public Safety and Corrections, accessed January 25, 2022, https://doc.louisiana.gov/about-the-dpsc.

30. Mission Statement Page, Yale University, accessed January 25, 2022, https://www.yale.edu/about-yale/mission-statement.

31. Mission & Objectives Page, University of Alabama, accessed January 25, 2022, https://www.ua.edu/about/mission.

32. Our Mission Page, Brigham Young University, accessed January 25, 2022, https://byucougars.com/page/our-mission-0.

33. About SNHU Page, Southern New Hampshire University, accessed January 25, 2022, https://www.snhu.edu/about-us.

34. Richard Chaitt, "College Mission Statements," *Science* 205, no. 4410 (September 7, 1979): 957, https://www.science.org/doi/10.1126/science.205.4410.957.

35. Laura McKenna, "The Madness of College Basketball Coaches' Salaries," *Atlantic*, March 24, 2016, https://www.theatlantic.com/education/archive/2016/03/the-madness-of-college-basketball-coaches-salaries/475146/.

36. "Quick Facts: Alabama," United States Census Bureau, accessed April 22, 2022, https://www.census.gov/quickfacts/AL; "Students by Race and Ethnicity," Office of Institutional Research and Assessment, accessed April 22, 2022, https://oira.ua.edu/factbook/reports/student-enrollment/fall-term/students-by-race-and-ethnicity/.

37. "Governor's Proposed State Budget 2021-22 Snapshot," Council on Criminal Justice and Behavioral Health, https://www.cdcr.ca.gov/ccjbh/wp-content/uploads/sites/172/2021/03/CCJBH_2021-22_Proposed_Budget_Snapshot-Final.pdf.

38. "Vision, Mission, Values, and Goals," California Department of Corrections and Rehabilitation, accessed April 22, 2022, https://www.cdcr.ca.gov/about-cdcr/vision-mission-values.

39. Lucius Couloute and Daniel Kopf, "Out of Prison & Out of Work: Unemployment Among Formerly Incarcerated People," Prison Policy Initiative, July 2018, https://www.prisonpolicy.org/reports/outofwork.html.

40. Lucius Couloute, "Nowhere to Go: Homelessness Among Formerly Incarcerated People," Prison Policy Initiative, August 2018, https://www.prisonpolicy.org/reports/housing.html.

41. "Recidivism and Reentry," Prison Policy Initiative, accessed March 4, 2022, https://www.prisonpolicy.org/research/recidivism_and_reentry/.

42. "Annual Determination of Average Cost of Incarceration Fee (COIF)," Federal Register, September 1, 2021, https://www.federalregister.gov/documents/2021/09/01/2021-18800/annual-determination-of-average-cost-of-incarceration-fee-coif.

43. "Higher Education: Students Need More Information to Help Reduce Challenges in Transferring College Credits," U.S. Government General Accountability Office, August 14, 2017, https://www.gao.gov/products/gao-17-574.

44. Paul LeBlanc, *Students First: Equity, Access, and Opportunity in Higher Education* (Cambridge, MA: Harvard Education Press, 2021).

45. Will Jarvis, "LSU Just Unveiled a $28-Million Football Facility. The Flood-Damaged Library Is Still 'Decrepit,'" *Chronicle of Higher Education*, July 22, 2019, https://www.chronicle.com/article/lsu-just-unveiled-a-28-million-football-facility-the-flood-damaged-library-is-still-decrepit.

46. Jim Engster, "Engster: LSU Fully Integrated 45 Years After Last All-White Team," *Tiger Rag*, August 1, 2016, https://www.tigerrag.com/engster-lsu-fully-integrated-45-years-after-last-all-white-team.

47. Peter Wagner and Wanda Bertram, "'What Percent of the U.S. Is Incarcerated?' (And Other Ways to Measure Mass Incarceration)," Prison Policy Initiative, January 16, 2020, https://www.prisonpolicy .org/blog/2020/01/16/percent-incarcerated.

48. "Social Welfare under Reagan," CQ Researcher, March 9, 1984, https://library.cqpress.com/cqresearcher/document.php?id=cqresrre 1984030900.

49. Matt Richtel, "How the Pandemic Is Imperiling a Working-Class College," *New York Times,* December 28, 2020, https://www.nytimes .com/2020/12/28/us/college-coronavirus-tuition.html.

50. Pamela Herd and Donald P. Moynihan, *Administrative Burden: Policy-making by Other Means* (New York: Russell Sage Foundation, 2019), 34.

51. Herd and Moynihan, 26.

52. Herd and Moynihan, 215–16.

53. Emily Henderson, "Hygienists Brace for Pitched Battles with Dentists in Fights over Practice Laws," News Medical, October 19, 2020, https://www.news-medical.net/news/20211019/Hygienists-brace-for -pitched-battles-with-dentists-in-fights-over-practice-laws.aspx.

54. Ariel Gelrud Shiro and Richard V. Reeves, "The For-Profit College System Is Broken and the Biden Administration Needs to Fix It," Brookings Institution, January 12, 2021, https://www.brookings.edu /blog/how-we-rise/2021/01/12/the-for-profit-college-system-is-broken -and-the-biden-administration-needs-to-fix-it.

55. Kara Gotsch and Vinay Basti, "Capitalizing on Mass Incarceration: U.S. Growth in Private Prisons," The Sentencing Project, August 2, 2018, https://www.sentencingproject.org/publications/capitalizing-on -mass-incarceration-u-s-growth-in-private-prisons.

56. Gotsch and Basti, "Capitalizing on Mass Incarceration"

57. Lisa Dodson, *The Moral Underground: How Ordinary Americans Subvert an Unfair Economy* (New York: The New Press, 2011).

58. Hamel and Zanini, 174–75.

59. Hamel and Zanini, 174–75.

60. James Vaznis, "Disengaged Workers at Boston Public Schools Are 'Busy Acting Out Their Unhappiness' and Undermining Colleagues, Survey Finds," *Boston Globe*, June 24, 2021, https://www.bostonglobe.com/2021/06/24/metro/disengaged-workers-boston-public-schools-are-busy-acting-out-their-unhappiness-undermining-colleagues-survey-finds.

61. Jessica Benjamin, "Non-Violence as Respect for All Suffering: Thoughts Inspired by Eyad El Sarraj," *Psychoanalysis, Culture, & Society*, 21 (2016): 8, https://link.springer.com/article/10.1057/pcs.2015.60.

62. Benjamin, 8.

63. Joshua M. Hayes, "What's the Difference Between a Public Benefit Corporation and a B Corp Certification?" *Hutchison* (blog), November 13, 2019, https://www.hutchlaw.com/blog/whats-the-difference-between-a-public-benefit-corporation-and-a-b-corp-certification.

64. "Business Roundtable Redefines the Purpose of a Corporation to Promote 'An Economy That Serves All Americans,'" *Business Roundtable*, August 19, 2019, https://www.businessroundtable.org/business-roundtable-redefines-the-purpose-of-a-corporation-to-promote-an-economy-that-serves-all-americans.

65. Carl Benedikt Frey and Michael A. Osborne, "The Future of Employment: How Susceptible Are Jobs to Computerization?" *Oxford Martin Programme on Technology and Employment*, September 17, 2013, https://www.oxfordmartin.ox.ac.uk/downloads/academic/The_Future_of_Employment.pdf.

66. Susan Lund, Anu Madgavkar, James Manyika, Sven Smit, Kweilin Ellingrud, and Olivia Robinson, "The Future of Work After COVID-19," *McKinsey Global Institute*, February 18, 2021, https://www.mckinsey.com/featured-insights/future-of-work/the-future-of-work-after-covid-19.

67. "Map: The Most Common Job in Every State," NPR, February 5, 2015, https://www.npr.org/sections/money/2015/02/05/382664837/map-the-most-common-job-in-every-state.

68. Kevin J. Delaney, "The Robot That Takes Your Job Should Pay Taxes, Says Bill Gates," Quartz, February 17, 2017, https://qz.com/911968/bill-gates-the-robot-that-takes-your-job-should-pay-taxes/.

69. Steven Botticelli, "Weak Ties, Slight Claims: The Psychotherapy Relationship in an Era of Reduced Expectations," *Contemporary Psychoanalysis* 48, no. 3 (2012): 563–576, https://doi.org/10.1080/00107530.2012.10746510.

70. Monica Anderson, Colleen McClain, Michelle Faverio, and Risa Gelles-Watnick, "The State of Gig Work in 2021," Pew Research Center, December 8, 2021, https://www.pewresearch.org/internet/2021/12/08/the-state-of-gig-work-in-2021/.

71. Botticelli, 566–567.

The Heart of Leadership

1. Michael H. McCain, "We Need a New Charter for Capitalism, and Here's What It Should Include," *Financial Post*, January 14, 2022, https://financialpost.com/news/economy/michael-h-mccain-we-need-a-new-charter-for-capitalism-and-heres-what-it-should-include.

2. Suzanne Simard, *Finding the Mother Tree: Discovering the Wisdom of the Forest* (New York: Knopf, 2021), 4.

3. Josh Gabbatis, "Can the Wood-Wide Web Really Help Trees Talk to Each Other?" *Science Focus*, May 15, 2020, https: //www.sciencefocus.com/nature/mycorrhizal-networks-wood-wide-web/.

4. Simard, 6.

5. Simard, 5.

6. C. Peterson and N. Park, "Character Strengths in Organizations," *Journal of Organizational Behavior* 27, no. 8 (2006): 1151, https://doi.org/10.1002/job.398.

7. Patrice Taddonio, "Trump the 'Bully': How Childhood & Military School Shaped the Future President," *Frontline*, September 22, 2020, https://www.pbs.org/wgbh/frontline/article/trump-the-bully-how-childhood-military-school-shaped-the-future-president/.

8. Doug Meyer, "Leadership Starts with . . . Love?" *The Company Leader*, December 27, 2017, http://companyleader.themilitaryleader.com/2017/12/27/leadership-start-love.

9. Edward A. Shils and Morris Janowitz, "Cohesion and Disintegration in the Wehrmacht in World War II," *The Public Opinion Quarterly* 12, no. 2 (Summer 1948): 280–315.

10. Frances Frei and Anne Morriss, *Unleashed: The Unapologetic Leader's Guide to Empowering Everyone Around You* (Boston: Harvard Business Review Press, 2020), 5.

11. Frei and Morriss, 4.

12. Gary Trosclair, "The Role of Community in Individuation," *The NYAAP* (blog), accessed March 7, 2022, https://nyaap.org/the-role-of-community-in-individuation.

INDEX

ABOUT THE AUTHOR

D r. Paul J. LeBlanc is President of Southern New Hampshire University (SNHU). Since 2003, under Paul's leadership, SNHU has grown from 2,800 students to over 180,000 learners and is the largest nonprofit provider of online higher education in the country.

The university was #12 on *Fast Company* magazine's "World's Fifty Most Innovative Companies" list and was the only university included. *Forbes Magazine* has listed him as one of its fifteen "Classroom Revolutionaries" and one of the "most influential people in higher education." *Washington Monthly* named him one of America's ten most innovative university presidents. In 2018, Paul won the prestigious TIAA Institute Hesburgh Award for Leadership Excellence in Higher Education, joining some of the most respected university and college presidents in American higher education.

Paul served as Senior Policy Advisor to Under Secretary Ted Mitchell at the U.S. Department of Education, working on competency-based education, new accreditation pathways, and innovation. He serves on the National Advisory Committee on Institutional Quality and Integrity (NACIQI) and on the National Academies of Sciences, Engineering and Medicine's Board on Higher Education and Workforce (and served on its Committee on Quality in Undergraduate Education). He also serves on the ACE Board and chairs the AGB Council of Presidents.

Paul immigrated to the United States as a child; was the first person in his extended family to attend college; and is a graduate of Framingham State University (BA), Boston College (MA), and the University of Massachusetts (PhD). From 1993 to 1996 he directed a technology startup for Houghton Mifflin Publishing Company, he was President of Marlboro College (VT) from 1996 to 2003, and he became President of SNHU in 2003. His wife, Patricia, is an attorney, and they have two daughters, Emma and Hannah.